LEVEL I AND II REFRESHER: CONTENTS

SCHWESERNOTES™ 2012 CFA LEVEL I AND II REFRESHER

©2011 Kaplan, Inc. All rights reserved.

Published in 2011 by Kaplan Schweser.

Printed in the United States of America.

ISBN: 978-1-4277-3609-3 / 1-4277-3609-X

PPN: 3200-1740

If this book does not have the hologram with the Kaplan Schweser logo on the back cover, it was distributed without permission of Kaplan Schweser, a Division of Kaplan, Inc., and is in direct violation of global copyright laws. Your assistance in pursuing potential violators of this law is greatly appreciated.

Required CFA Institute® disclaimer: "CFA® and Chartered Financial Analyst® are trademarks owned by CFA Institute. CFA Institute (formerly the Association for Investment Management and Research) does not endorse, promote, review, or warrant the accuracy of the products or services offered by Kaplan Schweser."

Certain materials contained within this text are the copyrighted property of CFA Institute. The following is the copyright disclosure for these materials: "Copyright, 2012, CFA Institute. Reproduced and republished from 2012 Learning Outcome Statements, Level I, II, and III questions from CFA® Program Materials, CFA Institute Standards of Professional Conduct, and CFA Institute's Global Investment Performance Standards with permission from CFA Institute. All Rights Reserved."

These materials may not be copied without written permission from the author. The unauthorized duplication of these notes is a violation of global copyright laws and the CFA Institute Code of Ethics. Your assistance in pursuing potential violators of this law is greatly appreciated.

Disclaimer: The Schweser Notes should be used in conjunction with the original readings as set forth by CFA Institute in their 2012 CFA Level III Study Guide. The information contained in these Notes covers topics contained in the readings referenced by CFA Institute and is believed to be accurate. However, their accuracy cannot be guaranteed nor is any warranty conveyed as to your ultimate exam success. The authors of the referenced readings have not endorsed or sponsored these Notes.

FOREWORD

This book contains a review of topics from Levels I and II that will help provide a foundation for studying for Level III. These are topics that the CFA Institute curriculum committee assumes you have already mastered when you study the Level III curriculum.

I have always told my Level III candidates, "Level I is foundation; Level II is valuation; Level III is application." At Level I, you saw a vast amount of material across many disciplines. Level I provides the general knowledge base any successful portfolio manager must have. Level II expands upon Level I and adds some fairly difficult valuation techniques used by successful portfolio managers. Once you have conquered Levels I and II, you are ready for the final challenge—putting together all you have learned with many new portfolio management techniques in Level III. In other words, you have been preparing for Level III since you started the CFA Program.

It is important to mention that the format of the Level III exam is different from Levels I and II. As you know, the Level I exam contains 240 multiple-choice questions. Although the questions are grouped according to topic area, each individual question is free-standing. The Level II exam contains 20 item sets. With item sets, you first saw questions grouped by a common scenario.

Just like the Level II exam, the afternoon session of the Level III exam contains ten 6-question item sets. The morning session of the Level III exam, however, contains about ten essay (constructed response essay) questions, each containing multiple parts. Some of the individual parts will be free-standing, but others will use the answer from a previous question as an input. This is known as double jeopardy—if you miss the first one, you miss the second one!

The Level III CFA Exam is a grueling mental (as well as physical) challenge that is not to be taken lightly. However, your hard work and dedication, combined with our high-quality study materials, are your key to exam day success. I wish you all the best for your studies at Level III.

Regards,

Bruce Kuhlman

Bruce Kuhlman, Ph.D., CFA, CAIA
Vice President and Level III Manager, Kaplan Schweser

LEVEL I AND II REFRESHER

QUANTITATIVE METHODS

Professor's Note: Quantitative Methods was completely removed from the Level III curriculum in 2008. The following material is presented for your review only. None of this material will necessarily be tested directly as it is, but some portfolio management topics assume you are familiar with these concepts.

Skewness and Kurtosis

Skewness represents the extent to which a distribution is not symmetrical.

A *right-skewed* distribution has positive skew (or skewness) and a mean that is greater than the median, which is greater than the mode.

A *left-skewed* distribution has negative skewness and a mean that is less than the median, which is less than the mode.

The attributes of normal and skewed distributions are summarized in the following illustration.

©2011 Kaplan, Inc.

Figure 1: Skewed Distributions

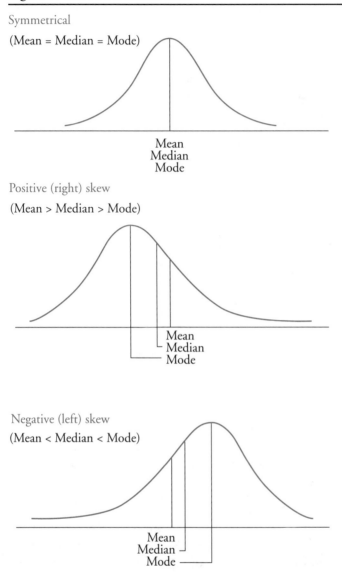

Symmetrical
(Mean = Median = Mode)

Mean
Median
Mode

Positive (right) skew
(Mean > Median > Mode)

Mean
Median
Mode

Negative (left) skew
(Mean < Median < Mode)

Mean
Median
Mode

To remember the relations, think of pulling on the end of a normal distribution, which is symmetrical with the mean, median, and mode equal. If you pull on the right or positive end, you get a right-skewed (positively skewed) distribution. If you can remember that adding extreme values at one end of the distribution has the greatest effect on the mean and doesn't affect the mode or high point of the distribution, you can remember the relations illustrated in the preceding graph.

Kurtosis is a measure of the degree to which a distribution is more or less peaked than a normal distribution, which has kurtosis of 3.

Excess kurtosis is kurtosis measured relative to that of a normal distribution. A distribution with kurtosis of 4 has excess kurtosis of 1. It is said to have positive excess kurtosis. A distribution with positive excess kurtosis (a leptokurtic distribution) will have more returns clustered around the mean and more returns with large deviations from the mean (fatter tails). In finance, positive excess kurtosis is a significant issue in risk assessment and management because fatter tails means an increased probability of extreme outcomes, which translates into greater risk.

Figure 2 illustrates the relative shapes of a normal and a leptokurtic distribution.

Figure 2: Kurtosis

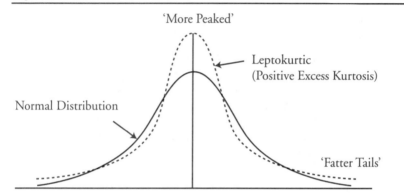

Covariance

The *covariance* between two variables is a measure of the degree to which the two variables move together. It measures the degree of linear relationship between two variables.

A *positive covariance* indicates that the variables tend to move together; a *negative covariance* indicates that the variables tend to move in opposite directions relative to their means. Covariance only indicates the direction of the relationship and does not measure the strength of the relationship. Therefore, if you compare the covariance measures for two sets of (paired) random variables and the second is twice the value of the first, the relationship of the second set isn't necessarily twice as strong as the first because the variance of the variables may be quite different as well.

©2011 Kaplan, Inc.

Correlation

The *correlation coefficient,* ρ, is a standardized measure (unlike covariances) of the strength of the linear relationship (correlation) between two variables. The correlation coefficient can range from −1 to +1.

$$\rho = \text{corr}(i, j) = \frac{\text{Cov}(i, j)}{\sigma_i \sigma_j}$$

Expected Return and Variance of a Portfolio of Two Stocks

The *expected return* and *variance of a portfolio of two assets* are calculated as:

$$\hat{R}_p = w_A R_A + w_B R_B$$

$$\sigma_p^2 = w_A^2 \sigma_A^2 + w_B^2 \sigma_B^2 + 2 w_A w_B \sigma_A \sigma_B \rho_{A,B}$$

$$\sigma_p^2 = w_A^2 \sigma_A^2 + w_B^2 \sigma_B^2 + 2 w_A w_B \text{Cov}_{A,B}$$

Note that $\sigma_A \sigma_B \rho_{A,B} = \text{Cov}_{A,B}$ so the formula can be written either way.

Confidence Intervals: Normal Distribution

A *confidence interval* is a range of values around an expected outcome within which we expect the actual outcome to occur some specified percentage of the time.

The following graph illustrates confidence intervals for a standard normal distribution, which has a mean of 0 and a standard deviation of 1. We can interpret the values on the x-axis as the number of standard deviations from the mean. Thus, for any normal distribution we can say, for example, that 68% of the outcomes will be within one standard deviation of the mean. This would be referred to as a 68% confidence interval.

Figure 3: The Standard Normal Distribution and Confidence Intervals

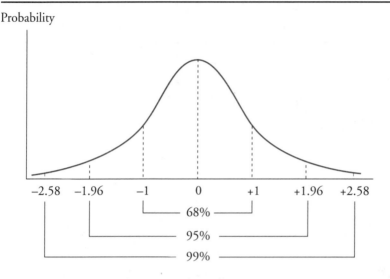

Shortfall Risk and Safety-First Ratio

Shortfall risk. The probability that a portfolio's return or value will be below a specified (target) return or value.

Roy's safety-first criterion. States that the optimal portfolio minimizes the probability that the return of the portfolio falls below some minimum acceptable threshold level.

Roy's safety-first ratio is similar to the Sharpe ratio. In fact, the Sharpe ratio is a special case of Roy's ratio where the threshold level is the risk-free rate of return.

Under both the Sharpe and Roy criteria, the best portfolio is the one that has the largest ratio.

Central Limit Theorem

The *central limit theorem* of statistics states that in selecting simple random samples of size n from a *population* with a mean μ and a finite variance σ^2, the sampling distribution of the sample mean approaches a normal probability distribution with mean μ and a variance equal to σ^2/n as the sample size becomes large.

The central limit theorem is extremely useful because the normal distribution is relatively easy to apply to hypothesis testing and to the construction of confidence intervals.

 ©2011 Kaplan, Inc.

Specific inferences about the population mean can be made from the sample mean, *regardless of the population's distribution*, as long as the sample size is sufficiently large.

Student's *t*-Distribution

- Symmetrical (bell-shaped).
- Defined by single parameter, degrees of freedom (*df*), where df = n − 1 for hypothesis tests and confidence intervals involving a sample mean.
- Has fatter tails than a normal distribution; the lower the df, the fatter the tails and the wider the confidence interval around the sample mean for a given probability that the interval contains the true mean.
- As sample size (degrees of freedom) increases, the *t*-distribution approaches the normal distribution.

Student's t-distribution is similar in concept to the normal distribution in that it is bell-shaped and symmetrical about its mean. The *t-distribution* is appropriate when working with small samples (n < 30) from populations with *unknown variance* and normal, or approximately normal, distributions. It may also be appropriate to use the *t*-distribution when the population variance is unknown and the sample size is large enough that the central limit theorem will assure the sampling distribution is approximately normal.

Figure 4: Student's *t*-Distribution and Degrees of Freedom

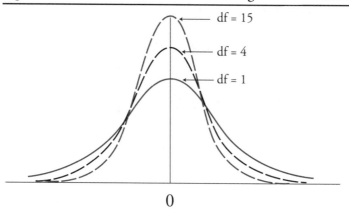

HYPOTHESIS TESTING

Hypothesis. Statement about a population parameter that is to be tested. For example, "The mean return on the S&P 500 Index is equal to zero."

©2011 Kaplan, Inc.

Steps in Hypothesis Testing

- State the hypothesis.
- Select a test statistic.
- Specify the level of significance.
- State the decision rule for the hypothesis.
- Collect the sample and calculate statistics.
- Make a decision about the hypothesis.
- Make a decision based on the test results.

Null and Alternative Hypotheses

The *null hypothesis*, designated as H_0, is the hypothesis the researcher wants to reject. It is the hypothesis that is actually tested and is the basis for the selection of the test statistics. Thus, if you believe (seek to show that) the mean return on the S&P 500 Index is different from zero, the null hypothesis will be that the mean return on the index *equals* zero.

The *alternative hypothesis*, designated H_a, is what is concluded if there is sufficient evidence to reject the null hypothesis. It is usually the alternative hypothesis you are really trying to support. Why? Because you can never really prove anything with statistics, when the null hypothesis is rejected, the implication is that the (mutually exclusive) alternative hypothesis is valid.

Two-Tailed and One-Tailed Tests

Two-tailed test. Use this type of test when testing a parameter to see if it is different from (not equal to) a specified value:

$$H_0: \mu = 0 \text{ versus } H_a: \mu \neq 0$$

Figure 5: Two-Tailed Test: Significance = 5%, Confidence = 95%

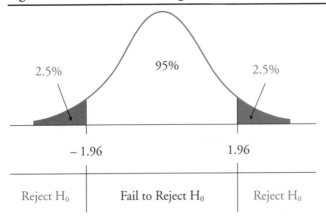

©2011 Kaplan, Inc.

One-tailed test. Use this type of test when testing a parameter to see if it is *above* or *below* a specified value:

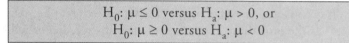

$$H_0: \mu \leq 0 \text{ versus } H_a: \mu > 0, \text{ or}$$
$$H_0: \mu \geq 0 \text{ versus } H_a: \mu < 0$$

With respect to the first hypothesis, $\mu \leq 0$, we will reject it only if the test statistic is significantly greater than zero (in the right-hand tail of the distribution). Thus, we call it a one-tailed test.

Figure 6: One-Tailed Test: Significance = 5%, Confidence = 95%

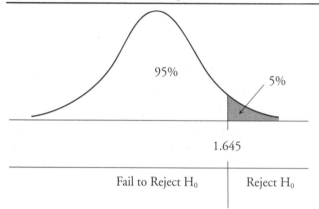

Test Statistic

A *test statistic* is calculated from sample data and is compared to a critical value to evaluate H_0. The most common test statistics are the z-statistic and the t-statistic. Which statistic you use to perform a hypothesis test will depend on the properties of the population and the sample size as previously noted.

- Critical values come from tables and are based on the researcher's desired level of significance. As the level of significance (the α) gets smaller, the critical value gets larger, and it becomes more difficult to reject the null hypothesis.
- If the test statistic exceeds the critical value (or is outside the range of critical values), the researcher rejects H_0.

Type I and Type II Errors

When testing a hypothesis, there are two possible types of errors:

- *Type I error.* The rejection of the null hypothesis when it is actually true.
- *Type II error.* The failure to reject the null hypothesis when it is actually false.

Significance Level (α)

The *significance level* is the probability of making a Type I error (i.e., rejecting the null when it is true) and is designated by the Greek letter alpha (α). You can think of this as the probability that the test statistic exceeded or fell below a critical value by chance. A significance level of 5% ($\alpha = 0.05$) means there is a 5% chance of incorrectly rejecting the null hypothesis.

TECHNICAL ANALYSIS

Technical analysis is the use of past price and trading volume data to forecast the future direction of prices. Technical analysts use charts to uncover *patterns* in prices and trading rules, such as relative strength and moving averages to compare current values to past or "normal" values.

Technical analysts more or less ignore the fundamentals of the company, market, currency, or commodity being analyzed. Instead, they base their decisions on charts of price and volume information and various other technical measures. Fundamental analysts, on the other hand, base projections on the fundamentals. Large brokerage houses and other financial institutions may have both technical and fundamental analysis teams.

Assumptions of Technical Analysis

- Values, and thus prices, are determined by supply and demand.
- Supply and demand is driven by both rational and *irrational* behavior.
- Security prices move in trends that persist for long periods of time.
- While the causes of changes in supply and demand are difficult to determine, the actual shifts in supply and demand can be observed in market price behavior.

Technical Analysis vs. Fundamental Analysis

One major difference between technical and fundamental analysis is the speed at which news is assumed to be impounded into market prices. Fundamentalists believe that prices react quickly to news, while technicians believe that the reaction is slow. Further, technicians look for change in supply and demand, while fundamentalists look for changes in value.

          ©2011 Kaplan, Inc.

Economics

Economic Growth

Labor Productivity and Productivity Curves

The two factors that contribute to labor productivity growth (real GDP per labor hour) are growth in physical capital per labor hour and technological change.

Productivity curves are a plot of labor productivity (y-axis) against capital per labor hour (x-axis) at a given state of technology, as shown in Figure 7.

Properties of productivity curves include the following:

- Productivity increases as capital per labor hour increases at a given state of technology. Growth in capital per labor hour causes movements along a productivity curve.
- Productivity increases as the state of technology increases at any given level of capital per labor hour. Technological growth causes productivity curves to shift.
- Productivity curves exhibit the law of diminishing returns.

Figure 7: Productivity Curve

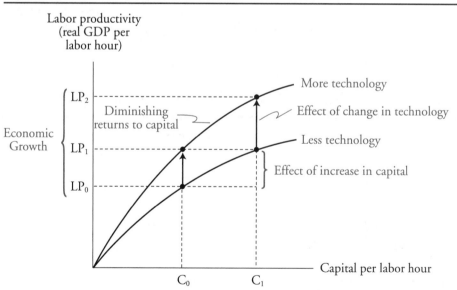

One-Third Rule

The one-third rule states that at a given level of technology, on average, a 1% increase in capital per labor hour results in a one-third of 1% increase in real GDP per labor hour. The one-third rule can be used to divide a change in productivity growth into two components: (1) that which is attributable to a change in capital per labor hour (i.e., movement along a productivity curve) and (2) that which is attributable to technological change (i.e., shifts in a productivity curve).

REGULATION AND ANTITRUST POLICY IN A GLOBALIZED ECONOMY

Economic Regulation

The main objective of economic regulation is to control the prices that the regulated firms are permitted to charge. There are two prevalent methods for economic regulation:

1. *Cost-of-service regulation* requires the producers in the regulated industry to charge prices based upon the actual average cost of producing the product or providing the service to the consumer.

2. *Rate-of-return regulation* permits producers in the regulated industry to formulate pricing policies that provide a competitive rate of return on their investment with no opportunities to earn a positive economic profit.

Negative Side Effects of Regulation

There can be unintended negative effects of regulation. A firm can conform to the letter, but not the intent, of the regulation through what is referred to as *creative response*. An example of a creative response is the *feedback effect*, which occurs when consumers' behavior is changed as a result of the new regulation.

Regulator Behavior

There are two predominant theories of regulators' behavior:

1. The *capture hypothesis* is based on the assumption that regardless of the reason why a regulatory agency was established, it will eventually be influenced or *captured* by the industry that is being regulated.

2. The *share-the-gains, share-the-pains theory* is based on the assumption that regulators will strive to satisfy all three interested parties: the legislators, the customers, and the regulated firms themselves.

   ©2011 Kaplan, Inc.

Costs of Regulation and Effects of Deregulation

Although beneficial in many ways, increased regulation leads to *higher costs* of production for the regulated industry, which in turn leads to higher prices for the end consumer. *Deregulation* typically has negative effects in the short term, but the long-run benefits include better service, more product variety, and lower costs.

TRADING WITH THE WORLD

A country has an absolute advantage in the production of a good if it can produce more of it than another country. A country may have an absolute advantage in the production of many or all goods relative to another country. This does not mean that they cannot gain from trade.

A country has a comparative advantage in the production of a good if its opportunity cost of producing that good (in terms of foregone production of other goods) is lower than that of another country. If a country has a comparative advantage in producing one good, the other country has a comparative advantage in producing another good.

As long as one country has a comparative advantage in producing some good, both countries can be made better off by trade.

Trade Restrictions

Trade restrictions are adopted to protect domestic industries and workers from foreign competition.

Reasons to restrict trade that have some support among economists are the following:

- To protect an industry necessary for national defense.
- To protect industries in the developmental stage (infant industries).
- To prevent a country from selling below cost to gain market share and damage domestic producers (anti-dumping).

Arguments for trade restrictions with very little support among economists are the following:

- Trade restrictions protect domestic jobs.
- Trade restrictions create domestic jobs.
- Trade with low-wage countries will depress domestic wage rates.

A *tariff* is a tax imposed on imports, while a *quota* is an import quantity limitation. Tariffs benefit domestic producers *and the domestic government* at the expense of domestic consumers and foreign producers.

Quotas benefit domestic producers at the expense of domestic consumers. Under a *quota*, unlike under a tariff, the domestic government does not receive any revenue.

Foreign firms often self-impose *voluntary export restraints* to avoid the imposition of tariffs and quotas.

INTERNATIONAL FINANCE

Supply and Demand in Foreign Exchange

Two factors determine the *demand for a currency*:

1. *Interest rate for deposits in the currency.* When a country's real interest rates increase (decrease) relative to real interest rates in other countries, demand for its currency increases (decreases).

2. *Expected future exchange rates.* If a currency is expected to appreciate (depreciate), it is more (less) attractive.

The same two factors affect the *supply of a currency*, with opposite effects to those on the demand for the currency. Because the same factors affect both supply and demand, exchange rates can be volatile even when the volume of transactions is not.

Parity Relationships

- *Purchasing power parity.* The same goods should cost the same in different countries once exchange rates have been factored in.
- *Interest rate parity.* Exchange rates must change such that the return on investments with the same level of risk is the same in any currency.

Central Bank Intervention

A central bank can intervene in the foreign exchange market as a buyer (increasing the demand for its currency) or as a seller (increasing the supply of its currency). Intervention can reduce short-run exchange rate volatility, but it cannot overcome genuine shifts in the equilibrium exchange rate.

FOREIGN EXCHANGE

Direct and Indirect Quotes

- *Direct quotes.* Domestic currency (DC) per foreign currency (FC): DC/FC.
- *Indirect quotes.* Foreign currency per domestic currency: FC/DC.

            ©2011 Kaplan, Inc.

Spot Rates and Forward Rates

- *Spot rates* are exchange rates for immediate delivery of the currency.
- *Forward rates* are exchange rates for currency transactions that will occur in the future.

Forward Discounts and Forward Premiums

The forward premium or discount is frequently stated as a percentage of the spot rate and can be *annualized* (using direct quotes) using the following formula:

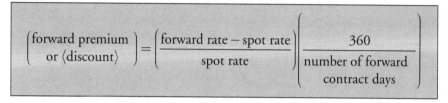

$$\begin{pmatrix} \text{forward premium} \\ \text{or } \langle\text{discount}\rangle \end{pmatrix} = \begin{pmatrix} \dfrac{\text{forward rate} - \text{spot rate}}{\text{spot rate}} \end{pmatrix} \begin{pmatrix} \dfrac{360}{\text{number of forward} \atop \text{contract days}} \end{pmatrix}$$

Using direct quotes, a foreign currency is at a forward premium (discount) if the forward price is greater (less) than the spot price.

For example, if the spot rate for Mexican pesos is $0.0893 and the forward rate is $0.0885, the peso is trading at a forward discount. The peso is expected to depreciate relative to the USD (i.e., it will be cheaper in the future).

The bid-ask spread on forward contracts will widen as currency volatility and contract maturity increase.

Interest Rate Parity

Covered interest rate parity, or simply **interest rate parity** (IRP), shows that there is a relationship between the spot and forward exchange rates and the domestic (r_{DC}) and foreign (r_{FC}) interest rates in the countries represented. Covered means that the currency exposure in the foreign investment is hedged or covered by a forward contract.

IRP is approximated by equating the difference between the domestic interest rate and the foreign interest rate to the forward premium or discount:

interest differential ≈ forward differential

Restating this relationship in more familiar terms gives:

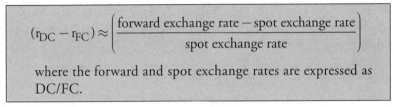

$$(r_{DC} - r_{FC}) \approx \left(\frac{\text{forward exchange rate} - \text{spot exchange rate}}{\text{spot exchange rate}} \right)$$

where the forward and spot exchange rates are expressed as DC/FC.

When the above condition prevails, equilibrium exists in the international money markets.

You should also know that the exact IRP equation using direct quotes is:

$$\frac{\text{forward}}{\text{spot}} = \left(\frac{1 + r_{DC}}{1 + r_{FC}} \right)$$

Covered Interest Arbitrage

Covered interest arbitrage is a trading strategy that exploits currency positions when the interest rate parity equation is not satisfied. The covered interest differential can be viewed by rewriting IRP in the following way:

$$1 + r_{DC} = \frac{(1 + r_{FC})(\text{forward rate})}{\text{spot rate}}$$

The left-hand side of the equation is the domestic interest rate, while the right-hand side is the hedged foreign rate (the foreign rate expressed in domestic terms). Arbitrage will prevent this relationship from getting out of line. To preclude arbitrage, the left-hand side minus the right-hand side should equal zero. Hence, the *covered interest differential* can be written as:

$$\text{covered interest differential} = (1 + r_{DC}) - \left(\frac{(1 + r_{FC})(\text{forward rate})}{\text{spot rate}} \right)$$

For example, if the domestic interest rate is less than the hedged foreign interest rate, an arbitrageur will borrow in the domestic cash market, buy foreign currency at the spot rate, and enter into a forward contract, granting him the ability to convert the foreign funds back to domestic funds at some future date. The foreign funds are invested at the foreign interest rate until the forward contract expires, at which time the arbitrageur will convert the proceeds from the foreign investment back into the domestic currency via the forward contract. This results in an arbitrage (riskless) profit with no net investment.

 ©2011 Kaplan, Inc.

FOREIGN EXCHANGE PARITY RELATIONS

Currency Appreciation or Depreciation

There are *three major factors* that cause a country's currency to appreciate or depreciate.

1. *Differences in income growth* among nations will cause nations with the highest income growth to demand more imported goods. The heightened demand for imports will increase demand for foreign currencies, appreciating the foreign currencies relative to the domestic currency.

2. *Differences in inflation rates* will cause the residents of the country with the highest inflation rate to demand more imported (cheaper) goods. If a country's inflation rate is higher than its trading partner's, the demand for the country's currency will be low, and the currency will depreciate.

3. *Differences in real interest rates* will cause a flow of capital into those countries with the highest available *real* rates of interest. Therefore, there will be an increased demand for those currencies, and they will appreciate relative to those of countries whose available real rate of return is lower.

Monetary and Fiscal Policy and Exchange Rates

Because monetary and fiscal policies exert an impact on income growth, inflation, and real interest rates, they will also influence exchange rates.

In the short run, a shift to an *expansionary monetary policy* (when the effects are not well anticipated) will lead to the following:

- More *rapid economic growth* (stimulates imports).
- An *accelerated inflation rate* (reduces exports by making domestic products more expensive).
- *Lower real interest rates* (reduces foreign investments).

Each of these factors increases the demand for foreign currencies relative to the domestic currency, causing the domestic currency to *depreciate*. Given a shift to a *restrictive monetary policy*, the *opposite* occurs.

The impact of *fiscal policy on exchange rates* is more complicated. A shift to a *more restrictive fiscal policy* will result in budget *surpluses*.

The reduced aggregate demand causes an economic slowdown and lower inflation. These factors discourage imports and encourage exports, resulting in a higher value of the domestic currency.

However, budget surpluses suggest that government borrowing declines, which reduces real rates and causes investment funds to flow out of the country. As a result, the value of the domestic currency tends to decline.

Because financial capital is mobile, the effect of the interest rate change generally dominates in the short run, leading to short-run depreciation. Given a shift to an expansionary fiscal policy, the opposite occurs.

Interest Rate Parity (IRP)

Interest rate parity describes the relationship that must exist between the current spot exchange rate and today's forward rate.

Exact methodology:

$$\frac{\text{forward rate}}{\text{spot rate}} = \frac{1 + \text{interest rate (DC)}}{1 + \text{interest rate (FC)}}$$

$$\text{forward discount / premium} = \frac{\text{interest rate (DC)} - \text{interest rate (FC)}}{1 + \text{interest rate (FC)}}$$

Spot and forward rates are expressed as DC/FC.

Linear approximation:

$$\text{forward premium or discount} \approx \text{interest rate (DC)} - \text{interest rate (FC)}$$

Important points to remember about IRP:

- Countries with high nominal interest rates *will* have their currencies sell at a forward discount.
- IRP must hold exactly (within transaction cost bounds) because investors will take advantage of interest rate differentials and earn arbitrage profits by moving funds between countries whose spot and forward exchange rates are not in balance.

The Asset Market Approach

According to the asset market approach, a sudden and unexpected *increase in the money supply of the domestic currency* will have offsetting short-run and long-run effects.

- In the short run, it will cause the domestic currency to depreciate. This is caused by an increase in expected inflation (equal to the percentage increase in the money supply) and a drop in domestic real interest rates.
- In the long run, the exchange rate will appreciate to the long-run, PPP-determined equilibrium level, and nominal interest rates will rise.

©2011 Kaplan, Inc.

CORPORATE FINANCE

CAPITAL BUDGETING

Capital budgeting is identifying and evaluating projects for which the cash flows extend over a period longer than a year. The process has four steps:

Step 1: Generating ideas.
Step 2: Analyzing project proposals.
Step 3: Creating the firm's capital budget.
Step 4: Monitoring decisions and conducting a post-audit.

Categories of capital budgeting projects include:

- Replacement projects to maintain the business.
- Replacement projects to reduce costs.
- Expansion projects to increase capacity.
- New product or market development.
- Mandatory projects, such as meeting safety or environmental regulations.
- Other projects, including high-risk research and development or management pet projects, are not easily analyzed through the capital budgeting process.

Five Key Principles of Capital Budgeting

1. Decisions are based on *incremental cash flows*. Sunk costs are not considered. Externalities, including *cannibalization* of sales of the firm's current products, should be included in the analysis.

2. Cash flows are based on *opportunity costs*, which are the cash flows the firm will lose by undertaking the project.

3. *Timing* of the cash flows is important.

4. Cash flows are analyzed on an *after-tax basis*.

5. *Financing costs* are reflected in the required rate of return on the project, not in the incremental cash flows.

Projects can be *independent* and evaluated separately, or *mutually exclusive*, which means the projects compete with each other and the firm can accept only one of them. In some cases, *project sequencing* requires projects to be undertaken in a certain order, with the accept/reject decision on the second project depending on the profitability of the first project.

A firm with *unlimited funds* can accept all profitable projects. However, when *capital rationing* is necessary, the firm must select the most valuable group of projects that can be funded with the limited capital resources available.

Capital Budgeting Methods

The *payback period* is the number of years it takes to recover the initial cost of the project. You must be given a maximum acceptable payback period for a project. This criterion ignores the time value of money and any cash flows beyond the payback period.

The *discounted payback period* is the number of years it takes to recover the initial investment in present value terms. The discount rate used is the project's cost of capital. This method incorporates the time value of money but ignores any cash flows beyond the discounted payback period.

The *profitability index* is the present value of a project's future cash flows divided by the initial cash outlay. The decision rule is to accept a project if its profitability index is greater than one, which is the same as the internal rate of return (IRR) > cost of capital rule and the net present value (NPV) > 0 rule (because PI = 1 + NPV/initial outlay).

Net present value for a normal project is the present value of all the expected future cash flows minus the initial cost of the project, using the project's cost of capital. A project that has a positive net present value should be accepted because it is expected to increase the value of the firm (shareholder wealth).

The *internal rate of return* is the discount rate that makes the present value of the expected future cash flows equal to the initial cost of the project. If the IRR is greater than the project's cost of capital, it should be accepted because it is expected to increase firm value. If the IRR is equal to the project's cost of capital, the NPV is zero.

For an independent project, the criteria for acceptance (NPV > 0 and IRR > project cost of capital) are equivalent and always lead to the same decision.

For mutually exclusive projects, the NPV and IRR decision rules can lead to different rankings because of differences in project size and/or differences in the timing of cash flows. The NPV criterion is theoretically preferred, as it directly estimates the effect of project acceptance on firm value.

Be certain you can calculate all these measures quickly and accurately with your calculator.

Because inflation is reflected in the weighted average cost of capital (WACC) (or project cost of capital) calculation, future cash flows must be adjusted upward to reflect positive expected inflation, or some wealth-increasing (positive NPV) projects will be rejected.

Larger firms, public companies, and firms where management has a higher level of education tend to use NPV and IRR analysis. Private companies and

©2011 Kaplan, Inc.

European firms tend to rely more on the payback period in capital budgeting decisions.

In theory, a positive NPV project should increase the company's stock price by the project's NPV per share. In reality, stock prices reflect investor expectations about a firm's ability to identify and execute positive NPV projects in the future.

COST OF CAPITAL

$$\text{WACC} = (w_d)[k_d(1 - t)] + (w_{ps})(k_{ps}) + (w_{ce})(k_{ce})$$

The proportions used for the three types of capital are target proportions and are calculated using market values. The WACC is used to compare the after-tax cost of raising capital to the expected after-tax returns on capital investments.

Cost of equity capital. There are three methods. You will likely know which to use by the information given in the problem.

1. CAPM approach: $\hat{R}_i = k_{ce} = R_F + \beta_i(\hat{R}_m - R_F)$.

2. Discounted cash flow approach: $k_{ce} = (D_1 / P_0) + g$.

3. Bond yield plus risk premium approach: k_{ce} = current market yield on the firm's long-term debt + risk premium.

Cost of preferred stock is calculated as follows:

$$k_{ps} = \frac{D_{ps}}{P}$$

Cost of debt is the average market yield on the firm's outstanding debt issues. Because interest is tax deductible, k_d is multiplied by $1 - t$.

Firm decisions about which projects to undertake are independent of the decision of how to finance firm assets at minimum cost. The firm will have long-run target weights for the percentages of common equity, preferred stock, and debt used to fund the firm. Investment decisions are based on a WACC that reflects each source of capital at its target weight, regardless of how a particular project will be financed or which capital source was most recently employed.

An analyst calculating a firm's WACC should use the firm's target capital structure, if known, or use the firm's current capital structure based on market values as the best indicator of its target capital structure. The analyst can incorporate trends in the company's capital structure into his estimate of the target structure. An alternative would be to apply the industry average capital structure to the firm.

CORPORATE GOVERNANCE OF LISTED COMPANIES

Corporate governance refers to the procedures, policies, and controls within a firm that determine how it is managed. In general, good corporate governance protects and advances shareholder interests and results in management acting ethically and legally and reporting accurate financial information in a timely manner.

Board members should be independent of management, not have other employment with the firm, be qualified/experienced, and be annually elected. The board itself should have the authority to hire outside consultants without management approval and have committees devoted to executive compensation, risk management, legal matters, and governance issues.

Shareholder rights should include proxy voting without attending the meeting, confidential voting, cumulative voting, approval over corporate structure changes, and ability to introduce proposals for board consideration. Shareholder rights are enhanced when there are not different classes of stock that separate economic ownership from voting rights.

A board should have a majority of independent members who do not have other relationships with management or the firm itself, and these members should regularly meet outside the presence of management. The audit committee of the board should be made up of independent members, be comprised of financial experts, have the authority to approve or reject any non-audit engagements of the auditor with the firm, and control the audit budget. Shareholders should have approval rights on the acceptance of the external auditor.

Members of the compensation committee should be independent and see that executive compensation is appropriate and tied to the long-term performance/ profitability of the firm. Shareholders should insist that the firm provide them with details regarding compensation, see that the terms and conditions of option grants are reasonable, and be alert to instances of option re-pricing.

In general, anti-takeover defenses benefit entrenched management and harm shareholders by decreasing share values.

 ©2011 Kaplan, Inc.

Equity Valuation

Valuation in Emerging Markets

How Inflation Affects Cash Flow Estimates

Cash flow forecasting for emerging market companies is challenging because emerging markets tend to experience high inflation levels, which makes the distinction between real and nominal cash flows and discount rates very important. Issues that require particular attention are:

- On the balance sheet inventory, plant, property, and equipment (non-monetary items) may be shown at values well below their current cost.
- On the income statement, depreciation charges will be well below replacement costs.

Recall the following definitions:

- NOPLAT = net operating profit less adjusted tax = EBIT − taxes.
- EBITDA = earnings before interest, taxes, depreciation, and amortization.
- FCInv = investment in fixed capital = capital expenditures.
- WCInv = investment in working capital = change in net working capital.

High inflation affects ratios calculated from nominal financial statements in the following manner:

- Sales growth will be overstated.
- Fixed asset turnover will be overstated, as fixed assets do not capture inflation effects in a timely manner but sales do reflect effect of inflation.
- Operating margins will be overstated, as sales reflect inflation but depreciation does not.
- Return on invested capital (NOPLAT / invested capital) is typically overstated, as NOPLAT is overstated and invested capital is understated.
- Solvency ratios, such as debt to assets, will be too high, as assets are understated.

The real valuation approach estimates value by discounting real cash flows at the real required return. The nominal valuation approach discounts nominal cash flows at the nominal discount rate.

The steps in valuing an emerging market's company on a real and nominal basis are:

1. Forecast real EBITDA and FCInv.

2. Forecast nominal depreciation, NOPLAT, FCInv, and WCInv.

3. Forecast real NOPLAT.

4. Forecast nominal and real free cash flows.

5.   Estimate firm value using a free cash flow model in both real and nominal terms by discounting real cash flows at the real WACC and nominal cash flows at the nominal WACC.

Incorporating Market Risk in Emerging Markets Valuation

There are two ways to incorporate emerging market risk into the valuation process:

1.   Adjust the cash flows in a probability-weighted scenario analysis and use a cost of capital estimated for emerging market companies. This is the preferred method because (1) country risks are diversifiable, (2) companies respond differently to country risk, (3) country risk is one-sided, and (4) identifying cash flow effects aids in risk management.

2.   Adjust the cost of capital by adding an ad hoc country risk premium and discount the unadjusted cash flows.

OVERVIEW OF DCF METHODS

Discounted cash flow (DCF) valuation is based on the idea that the value today of any security is the discounted value of all future cash flows. The general DCF methodology is applied in three separate, but highly related, frameworks.

Dividend discount models (DDMs). The DDM defines cash flow as dividends to be received in the future. This is based on the idea that, over time, earnings and dividends will converge. The DDM is most appropriate for mature and profitable firms that are not engaged in a fast-growing segment of the economy, or for large, diversified portfolios like the S&P 500. Use the DDM for valuation problems with the following characteristics:

•   The firm has a dividend history.
•   The dividend policy is consistent and related to earnings.
•   The perspective is that of a minority shareholder.

Free cash flow (FCF) *models.* Two versions of FCF valuation exist: FCF to the firm (FCFF) and FCF to equity (FCFE). FCFF is the cash flow generated by the firm above that required to maintain current operations. FCFE is FCFF minus the superior claims (i.e., creditors and preferred stockholders).

Residual income (RI). Residual income refers to the amount of earnings during the period that exceeds the investor's required earnings. Think of residual income as *economic profit*. In this framework, the value of the firm's equity is the firm's book value plus the present value of all future residual income. The RI method can be difficult to apply because it requires an in-depth analysis of the firm's accounting accruals.

                    ©2011 Kaplan, Inc.

The RI method is most appropriate under the following conditions:

- The firm does not have a dividend history.
- The firm's FCF is negative.
- It is a firm with transparent and high-quality accounting.

In all cases, you have to forecast the future cash flows (dividends, free cash flow, or residual income), determine the appropriate discount rate, and discount the cash flows to obtain the value of the firm. For the DDM, FCFE, and RI methods, the appropriate discount rate is the cost of equity. In general, there are three methods for determining the cost of equity:

1. The CAPM:

$$\hat{R}_i = R_F + \beta_i(\hat{R}_m - R_F)$$

2. The arbitrage pricing theory (APT), a multifactor model.

3. Adding a risk premium to the firm's bond yield.

For the FCFF model, the appropriate discount rate is the WACC.

Gordon Growth Model

The *Gordon growth model* assumes that dividends will grow at a constant rate forever. The formula is as follows:

$$V_0 = \frac{D_0(1+g)}{r-g} = \frac{D_1}{r-g}$$

The constant growth rate in dividends and earnings is g. Note that the value today, V_0, is dependent on the amount of the dividend one period from today, D_1. The model also assumes that r (the required return) is greater than g (the long-term, sustainable growth rate). You can solve the Gordon model for either r or g to determine the required return or growth rate implicit in the current market price.

The Gordon growth model is most appropriate for mature, stable firms. The limitations of the Gordon model include the following:

- Valuations are very sensitive to estimates of r and g.
- The model is difficult to apply to non-dividend-paying stocks.
- Unpredictable growth patterns from some firms make using the model difficult.

Two-Stage Growth Model

The multistage models are somewhat more complex. Basically, the multistage models (e.g., the 2-stage growth model and the H-model) *assume that there is some initial short-term growth period followed by a stable long-term growth period.* The 2-stage model assumes that the firm will experience a high rate of growth for the next few years followed by low growth for eternity.

The value of the stock is the present value of the dividends during the high-growth period plus the present value of the terminal value. The terminal value can be estimated using the Gordon growth model or a market multiple approach.

The Sustainable Growth Rate

The *sustainable growth rate* (SGR) is defined as the rate that earnings (and dividends) can continue to grow indefinitely, given that a firm's capital structure is unchanged and it doesn't issue any new equity. SGR can be derived from the relationship between the firm's retention rate and ROE as determined by the DuPont formula:

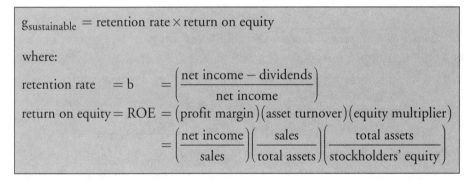

$$g_{sustainable} = \text{retention rate} \times \text{return on equity}$$

where:

$$\text{retention rate} = b = \left(\frac{\text{net income} - \text{dividends}}{\text{net income}}\right)$$

$$\text{return on equity} = ROE = (\text{profit margin})(\text{asset turnover})(\text{equity multiplier})$$

$$= \left(\frac{\text{net income}}{\text{sales}}\right)\left(\frac{\text{sales}}{\text{total assets}}\right)\left(\frac{\text{total assets}}{\text{stockholders' equity}}\right)$$

This has also been called the *PRAT model*, where SGR is a function of the profit margin (P), the retention rate (R), the asset turnover (A), and the degree of financial leverage (T). Unless otherwise instructed on the exam, use beginning-of-period balance sheet value to calculate SGR and to construct the DuPont model.

FREE CASH FLOW VALUATION

Free cash flow to the firm (FCFF) is the cash available to all the firm's investors, including common stockholders, preferred stockholders, and bondholders after the firm buys and sells products, provides services, pays its cash operating expenses, and makes short- and long-term investments. *Free cash flow to equity*

©2011 Kaplan, Inc.

(FCFE) is the cash available to the common stockholders after funding capital requirements, working capital needs, and debt financing requirements.

The FCFE/FCFF framework is analogous to the DDM framework. The main difference is that now we must be very careful to correctly calculate FCFF and FCFE from the income statement or the statement of cash flows, and we must make sure that we are using the correct discount rate (use the equity cost of capital with FCFE and the WACC with the FCFF).

Use the FCF model instead of DDM if the following conditions apply:

- The firm does not pay cash dividends.
- Dividend policy does not reflect the firm's long-run profitability.
- The firm is a take-over target (because FCF models take a control perspective).

Single-Stage FCFF/FCFE Models

Valuation using FCFF and FCFE is very similar to valuation using the DDMs. Let's begin with single-stage valuation. The formulas (which should look familiar) are as follows:

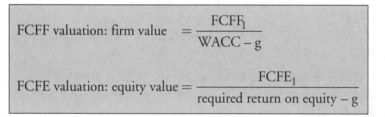

$$\text{FCFF valuation: firm value} = \frac{FCFF_1}{WACC - g}$$

$$\text{FCFE valuation: equity value} = \frac{FCFE_1}{\text{required return on equity} - g}$$

Note that to find the value of the firm today, the numerator is next year's FCF (i.e., $FCFF_1$ and $FCFE_1$). *It is imperative that you use the correct discount rate with the correct formula.* Because the FCFF framework values the entire firm, the cost of capital from all sources must be used (i.e., WACC). FCFE values only the cash flows that belong to equity holders; hence, the equity discount rate, r, is appropriate (think CAPM).

Two-Stage FCFF/FCFE Models

The 2-stage FCF framework is also analogous to the 2-stage DDM framework.

Remember the following steps:

Step 1: Chart the FCFs in high-growth period.

Step 2: Use single-stage FCF model to calculate terminal value at end of high-growth period.

Step 3: Discount interim FCF and terminal value to time zero to find value; use WACC with FCFF to find firm value; use required return on equity with FCFE to find equity value.

MARKET-BASED VALUATION: PRICE MULTIPLES

Price multiples are ratios of a common stock's market price to some fundamental variable. The most common example is the price-to-earnings (P/E) ratio. A **justified price multiple** (a.k.a. intrinsic P/E) is what the multiple *should be* if the stock is fairly valued. If the actual multiple is greater than the justified price multiple, the stock is overvalued; if the actual multiple is less than the justified multiple, the stock is undervalued (all else equal).

The Price-to-Earnings (P/E) Ratio

The most common market multiple is the P/E ratio. The main argument in favor of P/E valuation is that earnings power, as measured by EPS, is the primary determinant of investment value. There are a few problems with using the P/E ratio as a valuation tool:

- Earnings can be negative, which makes the P/E meaningless.
- The volatile, transitory portion of earnings makes the interpretation of P/Es difficult for analysts.
- Management has considerable discretion over accounting choices that affect reported earnings.

The P/E ratio can be calculated on a *leading* or *trailing basis*. On a trailing basis, earnings over the past 12 months are used in the denominator. With a leading basis, next year's expected earnings are used in the denominator.

While the price is always the market price of a share of stock, the analyst must determine the EPS. Analysts frequently use normalized EPS rather than EPS from the most recent financial statements. There are two methods of normalization:

1. *Historical average EPS.* The EPS in the P/E ratio is the historical average from the most recent complete business cycle.

2. *Average ROE.* The EPS in the P/E ratio is the average ROE over the most recent complete business cycle multiplied by the current book value per share.

 ©2011 Kaplan, Inc.

The PEG Ratio

The P/E to growth (PEG) ratio is equal to the ratio of the P/E multiple to earnings growth:

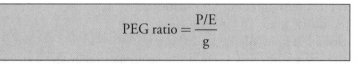

$$\text{PEG ratio} = \frac{P/E}{g}$$

The implied valuation rule is that stocks with lower PEG ratios are undervalued relative to high-PEG stocks, assuming similar risk.

The Price-to-Book (P/B) Ratio

The P/B ratio is calculated as the market price per share divided by the book value per share (common stockholders' equity = total assets – total liabilities – preferred stock). The *advantages* of the P/B ratio include:

- Book value is usually positive, even when earnings are negative.
- Book value is more stable than EPS.
- Book value is an appropriate measure of net asset value (especially for firms such as financial institutions that hold liquid assets).

The *disadvantages* of the P/B ratio are as follows:

- P/Bs can be misleading when there are significant size differences between firms.
- Book value is influenced by accounting choices/conventions.
- Inflation and technology can cause the book value and the market value of assets to differ significantly.

As with the P/E ratio, if we substitute into and rearrange the Gordon model, we can obtain a formula for the justified P/B:

$$\text{justified P/B} = \frac{\text{ROE} - g}{r - g}$$

The P/B increases as ROE increases. It also increases as the spread between ROE and *r* increases. Common adjustments to the book value include the exclusion of intangible assets, such as goodwill. Because the book value forecasts are not widely disseminated like EPS forecasts, analysts typically use trailing book value when calculating P/Bs.

The Price-to-Sales (P/S) Ratio

The P/S ratio is calculated by dividing the firm's stock price by revenue per share. The *advantages* of the P/S ratio include:

- The ratio is meaningful even for distressed firms.
- Sales revenue is not easily manipulated.
- P/S ratios are not as volatile as P/E ratios.
- P/S ratios are particularly useful in valuing mature, cyclical, and zero-income (start-up) firms.

The *disadvantages* of using the P/S ratio include:

- High sales do not necessarily mean high profits or cash flows.
- The P/S ratio does not capture differences in the cost structure between firms.
- Revenue recognition practices still distort sales.

REAL ESTATE

 Professor's Note: Real estate is tested as part of Alternative Investments at Level III.

The main value determinants, investment characteristics, principle risks, and most likely type of investor for the various classes of real estate are summarized in Figure 8.

Figure 8: Real Estate Investment Characteristics[1]

Investment	Factors That Affect Valuation	Principal Characteristics	Risk	Typical Investor
Raw land	• Supply/ demand. • Location. • Planning and zoning.	• Passive. • Illiquid. • Low leverage. • Return from value appreciation. • No tax depreciation. • Capital gains tax exposure. • Capitalized expenses.	• Cost of carry. • Unstable appreciation.	• Speculators/ developers. • Estates and long-term horizon portfolios.

---

1. Based on Figure 1 on pages 10–11, *Alternative Investments and Fixed Income*, CFA Program Curriculum, Volume 5, Level II (CFA Institute, 2012).

    ©2011 Kaplan, Inc.

Figure 8: Real Estate Investment Characteristics (Cont.)

Investment	Factors That Affect Valuation	Principal Characteristics	Risk	Typical Investor
Apartments	• Population growth. • Income growth. • Location. • Status.	• Moderately active. • Medium liquidity. • High leverage. • Return from income plus appreciation. • Tax depreciation. • Ordinary and capital gains tax exposure. • Inflation hedge.	• Start-up for new construction. • Hiring effective management for large investments.	• High income in need of tax shelter. • Anyone with sufficient initial equity requirement.
Office buildings	• Local economic expansion. • Location. • Tenant mix. • Favorable status.	• Active if more than one tenant. • Medium liquidity. • Moderate leverage. • Return from income plus appreciation. • Tax depreciation. • Ordinary and capital gains tax exposure.	• Start-up for new construction. • Hiring effective management for high service needs. • Competition. • Obsolescence. • Business activity location shifts.	• High income in need of tax shelter. • Anyone with sufficient initial equity; requirement if professional management is employed.
Warehouses	• Commercial/industrial activity. • Location. • Design for material handling change.	• Very passive. • Medium liquidity. • Medium leverage. • Return mostly from periodic income. • Tax depreciation. • Mostly ordinary income tax exposure.	• Oversupply. • Obsolescence when material handling procedures change.	• Retirees with desire for high cash flow, little management involvement. • Anyone in need of tax shelter with sufficient initial equity requirement.

Figure 8: Real Estate Investment Characteristics (Cont.)

Investment	Factors That Affect Valuation	Principal Characteristics	Risk	Typical Investor
Shopping centers	• Community growth. • Population and income. • Location. • Adequate parking. • Suitable tenant mix. • Lease terms.	• Moderately active. • Low liquidity. • Medium leverage. • Return from income plus appreciation. • Tax depreciation. • Ordinary and capital gains tax exposure.	• Establishing proper tenant mix at start-up. • Service-focused management needed. • High vacancy rate. • Competition. • Obsolescence.	• High wealth to make large equity outlay. • Anyone in need of tax shelter.
Hotels/ motels	• Location. • Demand by business and tourists. • Facility and service mix.	• Active. • Medium/low liquidity. • Medium/low leverage. • Return from income plus appreciation. • Tax depreciation. • Ordinary and capital gains tax exposure.	• Maintaining sufficient size. • Competent management. • Competition.	• Anyone in need of tax shelter with sufficient initial equity requirement. • Owner/ managers for smaller properties.

Valuing Real Estate Investments

You will not be asked to value a piece of real estate using the NPV and/or IRR methodologies, but both are fairly straightforward.

The *NPV* of a real estate investment may be expressed as the following:

$$NPV = \frac{CFAT_1}{\left(1+i_{at}\right)^1} + \frac{CFAT_2}{\left(1+i_{at}\right)^2} + ... + \frac{CFAT_n}{\left(1+i_{at}\right)^n} + \frac{ERAT}{\left(1+i_{at}\right)^n} - EI$$

where:
$CFAT_t$ = cash flow after taxes for period t
$ERAT$ = equity reversion after taxes (net equity at sale)
EI = initial equity investment in the property
i_{at} = risk-adjusted after-tax required return

©2011 Kaplan, Inc.

Decision rule: Undertake an investment only if its NPV is equal to or greater than zero.

The *IRR* for a real estate investment is the discount rate that makes the present value of a property's cash flow equal the amount of the equity investment (i.e., the IRR is the discount rate that makes the NPV of the real estate investment equal zero).

Decision rule: Undertake an investment if its IRR is equal to or greater than a specified required return or *hurdle rate.*

Problems Associated With Using IRR

Multiple IRRs. When the cash flows from a project change signs during the life of the investment, the IRR calculation may result in multiple solutions.

Ranking conflicts. When ranking mutually exclusive projects (i.e., only one of a set of possible investments may be accepted), NPV and IRR may yield different decisions due to the following:

- Relatively large differences in the sizes of the projects.
- Significantly different pattern or timing of the cash flows.

When conflict exists between the NPV and IRR decision recommendations, the project with the highest positive NPV should be accepted.

Fixed-Income Investments

Features of Debt Securities

Bond Terminology

- The terms under which money is borrowed are contained in an agreement known as the *indenture*. The indenture defines the obligations of and restrictions on the borrower and forms the basis for all future transactions between the lender/investor and the issuer. These terms are known as covenants and include both *negative* (prohibitions on the borrower) and *affirmative* (actions that the borrower promises to perform) sections.
- The *term to maturity* (or simply maturity) of a bond is the length of time until the loan contract or agreement expires. It defines the (remaining) life of the bond.
- The *par value* of a bond is the amount that the borrower promises to pay on or before the maturity date of the issue.
- The *coupon rate* is the rate that, when multiplied by the par value of a bond, gives the amount of interest to be paid annually by the borrower.

Coupon Structures

- *Zero-coupon bonds* are bonds that do not pay periodic interest. Such bonds do not carry coupons but instead are sold at a deep discount from their par values. Market convention dictates that semiannual compounding should be used when pricing zeros.
- *Accrual bonds* are similar to zero-coupon bonds but are sold originally at par value. There is a stated coupon rate, but the coupon interest builds up at a compound rate until maturity.
- *Step-up notes* have coupon rates that increase over time at a specified rate.
- *Deferred-coupon bonds* carry coupons, but the initial coupon payments are deferred for some period.

Floating-Rate Securities

- Floating-rate securities make varying coupon interest payments that are set based on a specified interest rate or index using the specified coupon formula:

> new coupon rate = reference rate ± quoted margin

- Some floating rate securities have limits on the coupon rate. An upper limit, which is called a *cap*, puts a maximum on the interest rate paid by the borrower. A lower limit, called a *floor*, puts a minimum on the interest rate received by the lender. When a bond has both a cap and a floor, the combination is called a *collar*.

©2011 Kaplan, Inc.

Accrued Interest and the Clean and Full Prices

When a bond is sold between coupon payment dates, part of the next coupon belongs to the seller. Normally, bond prices are quoted without accrued interest, and this is called the *clean price*. A bond price that includes accrued interest is called the *full price*.

Embedded Options

A *call feature* gives the issuer of a bond the right to retire the issue early by paying the call price, which is typically above the face value of the bond at the first call date and declines over time to par. A period of years after issuance for which there is no call allowed is called the period of *call protection*.

A *prepayment option* is similar to a call feature and gives the issuer of an amortizing (e.g., mortgage) security the right to repay principal ahead of scheduled repayment, in whole or in part.

A *put feature* gives the owner of a bond the right to receive principal repayment prior to maturity.

A *conversion option* gives a bondholder the right to exchange the bond for a specified number of common shares of the issuer. When such an option allows exchange for the common shares of another issuer, it is called an *exchange option*.

An *embedded option* that benefits the issuer will increase the yield required by bond buyers. An embedded option that benefits the bondholder will decrease the yield required on the bond.

Repurchase Agreements

A *repurchase (repo) agreement* is an arrangement by which an institution sells a security and commits to buy it back at a later date (*repurchase date*) at a predetermined price. The *repurchase price* is greater than the selling price and accounts for the interest charged by the buyer, who is essentially lending funds to the seller.

Most bond dealers finance inventories with repo agreements rather than with margin loans, which typically have higher rates and more restrictions.

RISKS ASSOCIATED WITH INVESTING IN BONDS

The most important risks associated with investing in bonds are interest rate risk, reinvestment risk, and credit risk.

Interest rate risk. As the rates go up (down), bond prices go down (up). This is the source of interest rate risk, which is approximated by *duration*.

Call risk. Call protection reduces call risk. When interest rates are more volatile, callable bonds have more call risk.

Prepayment risk. If rates fall, causing prepayments to increase, the investor must reinvest at the new lower rate.

Yield curve risk. Changes in the shape of the yield curve mean that yields change by different amounts for bonds with different maturities.

Reinvestment risk. Reinvestment risk occurs when interest rates decline and investors are forced to reinvest bond (or any other) cash flows at lower yields. Reinvestment risk is the greatest for bonds that have embedded call options, prepayment options, or high coupon rates and is greater for amortizing securities than for non-amortizing securities.

Credit risk. Credit risk comes in three forms—*default risk, credit spread risk,* and *downgrade risk.*

Liquidity risk. Because investors prefer more liquidity to less, a decrease in a security's liquidity will decrease its price, and the required yield will be higher.

Exchange-rate risk. This is the uncertainty about the value of foreign currency cash flows to an investor's home-country currency.

Volatility risk. This risk is present for fixed-income securities that have embedded options—call options, prepayment options, or put options. Changes in interest rate volatility affect the value of these options and thus affect the value of securities with embedded options.

Inflation risk. This is the risk of *unexpected* inflation, also called purchasing power risk.

Event risk. Risks outside the risks of financial markets (e.g., natural disasters, corporate takeovers).

©2011 Kaplan, Inc.

Bond Characteristics and Interest Rate Risk

Characteristic	Interest Rate Risk	Duration
Maturity ↑	Interest rate risk ↑	Duration ↑
Coupon ↑	Interest rate risk ↓	Duration ↓
Add a call	Interest rate risk ↓	Duration ↓
Add a put	Interest rate risk ↓	Duration ↓

Duration of a Bond

Duration is a measure of a security's price sensitivity to changes in yield. It can be interpreted as an approximation of the percentage change in the bond price for a 1% change in yield. It is the ratio of the percentage change in bond price to the change in yield in percent.

$$\text{duration} = -\frac{\%\text{ change in bond price}}{\%\text{ change in yield}}$$

To get the approximate percentage bond price change, given its duration and a specific change in yield, use the following formula:

$$\%\text{ change in bond price} = -\text{duration} \times \%\text{ change in yield}$$

Dollar duration is the approximate price change in dollars (or other currency) in response to a change in yield of 100 basis points (1%). With a duration of 5.2 and a market value of $1.2 million, we can calculate the dollar duration as 5.2% × $1.2 million = $62,400.

OVERVIEW OF BOND SECTORS AND INSTRUMENTS

Securities Issued by the U.S. Department of the Treasury

Treasury securities. Issued by the U.S. Treasury, thus backed by the full faith and credit of the U.S. government. Considered to be credit risk free.

Treasury bills. T-bills have maturities of less than one year and do not make explicit interest payments, paying only the face (par) value at the maturity date. They are sold at a discount to par, and interest is received when the par value is paid at maturity.

Treasury notes and Treasury bonds. Pay semiannual coupon interest at a rate that is fixed at issuance. Notes have original maturities of 2, 3, 5, and 10 years. Bonds have original maturities of 20 or 30 years.

Treasury inflation protected securities (TIPS). Coupon rate is fixed, but the face/principal value of the security is adjusted semiannually based on the change in the consumer price index (CPI). This inflation-adjusted principal is multiplied by the fixed-coupon rate to determine the interest payments to investors:

$$\text{coupon payment} = \text{inflation-adjusted par value} \times (\text{stated coupon rate} / 2)$$

Treasury STRIPS. Because the *U.S. Treasury does not issue zero-coupon notes and bonds*, investment bankers began stripping the coupons from Treasuries to create zero-coupon bonds to meet investor demand. Two types of these stripped securities are:

- *Coupon strips* are the coupon payments, each of which has been stripped from the original security and acts like a fixed-term zero-coupon bond.
- *Principal strips* refer to the principal payments from stripped bonds.

Federal agency securities. Agency bonds are debt securities issued by various agencies and organizations of the U.S. government, such as the Federal Home Loan Bank (FHLB). Most agency issues are not obligations of the U.S. Treasury and technically should not be considered to be riskless like Treasury securities. However, they are very high-quality securities that have almost no risk of default.

Mortgage Passthrough Securities

A *mortgage passthrough security* is created by pooling a large number of mortgages together. Shares are sold in the form of *participation certificates*. Interest, scheduled principal payments, and prepayments are passed through to investors after deducting small administrative and servicing fees. Like the underlying mortgage loans, mortgage passthroughs are *amortizing securities*. Prepayment risk is the risk that homeowners either pay additional principal or pay off the entire loan balance prior to the stated maturity. This typically happens when interest rates are low—so the investor gets more principal back in a low-interest-rate environment.

Collateralized mortgage obligations (CMOs) are created from mortgage passthrough securities. Different tranches (slices) represent claims to different cash flows from the passthrough securities and can have different maturities or different prepayment risk than the original passthrough.

    ©2011 Kaplan, Inc.

Securities Issued by Municipalities in the United States

The coupon interest on *municipal bonds* is typically exempt from federal taxation in the United States and from state income tax in the state of issuance. Two types of municipal bonds (munis) are:

- *Tax-backed debt* (general obligation bond) is secured by the full faith and credit of the borrower and is backed by its unlimited taxing authority, which includes the ability to impose individual income tax, sales tax, property tax, or corporate tax.
- *Revenue bonds* are supported only by the revenues generated from projects that are funded with the help of the original bond issue.

To compare tax-exempt with taxable bonds (like corporates), you must convert the tax-exempt yield to a taxable equivalent yield.

$$\text{taxable equivalent yield} = \frac{\text{tax-exempt municipal yield}}{1 - \text{marginal tax rate}}$$

Insured bonds are guaranteed for the life of the issue by a third party.

Pre-refunded bonds have been collateralized with Treasury securities in an amount sufficient to make scheduled interest and principal payments and are considered of the highest quality.

Corporate Bonds

Secured bonds have first claim to specific assets in the event of default.

Unsecured bonds are called *debentures*. Those with first claim to cash flows and to proceeds of asset sales in the event of liquidation are called *senior bonds*.

Junior bonds have a claim after those of senior bonds and are sometimes called *subordinated* bonds or notes. All bonds have priority to cash flows before those of preferred stock and common stock.

Asset-Backed Securities (ABS)

Asset-backed securities are collateralized by financial assets that the corporation has sold to a separate legal entity. They lower borrowing costs when the separate entity (special purpose vehicle) can attain a higher credit rating than the corporation.

With this structure, financial difficulties of the corporation should not affect the ABS credit. Often, credit enhancements in the form of guarantees of another corporation, a bank letter of credit, or bond insurance are employed to further reduce borrowing costs.

Other Debt Instruments

Negotiable CDs are issued in a wide range of maturities by banks, traded in a secondary market, backed by bank assets, and termed Eurodollar CDs when denominated in US$ and issued outside the United States.

Bankers acceptances are issued by banks to guarantee a future payment for goods shipped, are sold at a discount to the future payment they promise, are short term, and have limited liquidity.

Collateralized debt obligations (CDOs) are backed by an underlying pool of debt securities that may be any one of a number of types: corporate bonds, bank loans, emerging markets debt, mortgage-backed securities, or other CDOs.

The primary market in bonds includes underwritten and best-efforts public offerings, as well as private placements. The secondary market in bonds includes some trading on exchanges and a much larger volume of trading in the dealer [over-the-counter (OTC)] market. Electronic trading networks continue to be an increasingly important part of the secondary market for bonds.

YIELD SPREADS

Central Bank Interest Rate Policy Tools

In the United States, the Federal Reserve (Fed) manages short-term rates through the following *monetary policy tools*:

- *Discount rate.* Rate at which banks can borrow reserves from the Fed.
- *Open market operations.* Buying/selling of Treasury securities by the Fed in the open market. When the Fed buys securities, cash replaces securities in investor accounts, more funds are available for lending, and rates decrease. Sales of securities by the Fed have the opposite effect.
- *Bank reserve requirements.* By increasing the percentage of deposits banks are required to retain as reserves, the Fed effectively decreases the funds that are available for lending, which tends to increase rates.
- *Persuading banks to tighten or loosen their credit policies.*

 ©2011 Kaplan, Inc.

Theories of the Term Structure of Interest Rates

Pure expectations theory

Under this theory, the yield curve only reflects expectations about future short-term interest rates.

> short-term rates expected to rise in the future $\Rightarrow$ upward-sloping yield curve
> short-term rates expected to fall in the future $\Rightarrow$ downward-sloping yield curve
> short-term rates expected to rise then fall $\Rightarrow$ humped yield curve
> short-term rates expected to remain constant $\Rightarrow$ flat yield curve

Liquidity preference theory

Under this theory, the yield curve is upward sloping to reflect the fact that investors require a term premium that increases at longer maturities.

Market segmentation theory

Under this theory, lenders and borrowers have preferred maturity ranges, and the shape of the yield curve is determined by the supply and demand for securities within each maturity range.

Types of Yield Spreads

Nominal yield spreads measure the difference between the market yields on two bonds. Yield spreads can be caused by differences in credit quality, call features, tax treatment, or maturity.

- *Absolute yield spread.* Quantifies the difference between nominal yields on two bonds or two types of bonds. Calculated by:

$$\text{absolute yield spread} = \text{higher yield} - \text{lower yield}$$

  Typically, the yield spread is calculated between a non-Treasury security and a benchmark Treasury security of the same maturity.

- *Relative spread.* Quantifies the absolute spread as a percentage of the lower yield.

$$\text{relative yield spread} = \frac{\text{higher yield}}{\text{lower yield}} - 1$$

- *Yield ratio.* Calculated as:

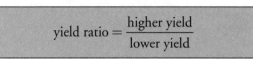

$$\text{yield ratio} = \frac{\text{higher yield}}{\text{lower yield}}$$

Credit Spreads

Credit spread refers to the difference in yield between two issues that are identical in all respects except their credit ratings. Credit spreads are a function of the economy's state. During economic expansion, credit spreads decline as corporations are expected to have stronger cash flows. During economic contractions, cash flows are pressured, which leads to a greater probability of default and increasing credit spreads.

Monetary Policy in Global Financial Markets

When the financial markets get new information that suggests inflation risks, how they react will depend on how well they understand and predict the central bank's policy response. If the central bank communicates its intentions poorly or makes policy decisions that surprise the markets, it will cause uncertainty and instability.

If the central bank's monetary policy actions are predictable, credible, and transparent, the markets will adjust quickly to expected changes in policy in response to events. Interest rates can reflect an expected policy action even before the central bank implements it. Overnight interest rates and short-term forward rates can be used to assess whether markets anticipate policy moves correctly.

Valuation of Fixed-Income Securities

Bond Valuation Process

- Estimate the cash flows over the life of the security—coupon payments and return of principal.
- Determine the appropriate discount rate based on risk associated with the estimated cash flows.
- Calculate the present value of the estimated cash flows.

Bond Valuation

Bond prices, established in the market, can be expressed either as a percentage of par value or as a yield. Yield to maturity (YTM) is the single discount rate that will make the present value of a bond's promised semiannual cash flows equal to the market price.

 ©2011 Kaplan, Inc.

In the United States, bonds typically make coupon payments (equal to one-half the stated coupon rate multiplied by the face value) twice a year, and the yield to maturity is expressed as twice the semiannual discount rate that will make the present value of the semiannual coupon payments equal to the market price. This non-compounded yield to maturity, calculated for a semiannual-pay bond, is also referred to as a *bond equivalent yield.*

For bonds that make annual payments, the YTM is the annual discount rate that makes the present value of the annual coupon payments equal to the market price. Thus, the relation between an annual and semiannual YTM is:

$$YTM_{\text{annual-pay}} = \left(1 + \frac{YTM_{\text{semiannual-pay}}}{2}\right)^2 - 1$$

$$YTM_{\text{semiannual-pay}} = \left[(1 + YTM_{\text{annual-pay}})^{\frac{1}{2}} - 1\right] \times 2$$

The relation between the semiannual YTM (the bond equivalent yield) and price for a bond with N years to maturity can be represented as:

$$\text{bond price} = \frac{CPN_1}{(1 + YTM/2)} + \frac{CPN_2}{(1 + YTM/2)^2} + \ldots + \frac{CPN_{2N} + \text{par}}{(1 + YTM/2)^{2N}}$$

The price-yield relationship for a zero-coupon bond with N years to maturity is based on a semiannual yield or bond equivalent yield by convention, so we have:

$$\text{zero-coupon bond price} = \frac{\text{face value}}{\left(1 + \dfrac{YTM}{2}\right)^{2N}}$$

$$\text{zero-coupon YTM} = \left[\left(\frac{\text{face value}}{\text{price}}\right)^{\frac{1}{2N}} - 1\right] \times 2$$

A bondholder will actually realize the YTM on an initial investment only if all payments are made as scheduled; the bond is held to maturity; and, importantly, all interim cash flows are reinvested at the YTM.

YIELD MEASURES, SPOT RATES, AND FORWARD RATES

Sources of Bond Return

- Periodic coupon interest payments.
- Recovery of principal, along with any capital gain or loss.
- Reinvestment income.

Traditional Measures of Yield

Current yield:

$$\text{current yield} = \frac{\text{annual coupon payment}}{\text{bond price}}$$

This measure looks at just one source of return: *a bond's annual interest income*; it does not consider capital gains/losses or reinvestment income.

The relationships between different yield measures are displayed in the following table:

Bond Selling at	Relationship
Par	coupon rate = current yield = yield to maturity
Discount	coupon rate < current yield < yield to maturity
Premium	coupon rate > current yield > yield to maturity

Yield to maturity, call, put, refunding:

Yields to other events besides maturity are calculated in the same way as YTM and are essentially internal rate of return measures. For example, to calculate the yield to call (YTC), we need to use the number of semiannual periods until the call date under consideration (for N) and the call price in place of the maturity value (for FV).

The key to YTC computations is using the right number of periods (to first call) and the appropriate terminal value (the call price).

          ©2011 Kaplan, Inc.

Bootstrapping Spot Rates

> **Example:**
>
> A 2-year bond with an 8% annual coupon is priced at 100, and the 1-year spot rate is 4%. Use the bootstrapping method to find the 2-year spot rate.
>
> **Answer:**
>
> The arbitrage-free pricing relationship is $100 = \dfrac{8}{1.04} + \dfrac{108}{\left(1+Z_2\right)^2}$,
>
> so we can write $100 - 7.6923 = \dfrac{108}{\left(1+Z_2\right)^2}$ and solve for Z_2 as
>
> $Z_2 = \left[\dfrac{108}{92.3077}\right]^{\frac{1}{2}} - 1 = 8.167\%.$

The idea of bootstrapping is that we can repeat this process sequentially. Given Z_1, Z_2, and the price of a 3-year bond, we could calculate Z_3 in the same manner.

Forward Rates

A *forward rate* is a rate for borrowing/lending at some date in the future. The key here is that investors should receive the same total return from investing in a 2-year bond as they would if they invested in a 1-year bond and then rolled the proceeds into a second 1-year bond at maturity of the first bond, one year from today.

We denote today's 1-year spot rate (the 1-year rate at which you could borrow or lend today) as $S_{0,1}$, where the first subscript denotes the starting point (on a time line) and the second subscript denotes the length of the spot rate. Looking at a time line, we could interpret this as the rate from 0 to 1. Likewise, $S_{0,3}$ would be the 3-year rate starting today (i.e., the rate from 0 to 3 on a time line).

We denote forward rates in much the same fashion, but forward rates are *expected* future spot rates. For example, $f_{1,1}$ can be defined as the 1-year forward rate starting in one year or as the *expected* 1-year spot rate starting in one year. Likewise, $F_{1,2}$ is the 2-year rate expected in one year, and $f_{2,1}$ is the 1-year rate expected in two years.

Professor's Note: Interest rate symbols and terminology can vary significantly from author to author, especially with respect to the interpretation or even the placement of the subscripts. Typically, however, capital letters are used to denote spot and multi-period forward interest rates, and lower case letters are used to denote 1-year forward rates.

Assuming a 5-year holding period and no expectations for changing interest rates, an investor should be indifferent between locking in the current 5-year rate, $S_{0,5}$, or locking in a series of short rates consisting of the current 1-year spot rate, $S_{0,1}$, and the remaining four 1-year forward rates.

The important implication of these relationships is that you can calculate any expected spot rate using combinations of spot and forward rates. For example, the current multi-year spot rate, $S_{0,N}$, can be expressed as the *geometric average* of the current 1-year spot and implied forward (i.e., expected spot) rates:

$$S_{0,N} = \left[(1+S_{0,1})(1+f_{1,1})(1+f_{1,2})...(1+f_{1,N}) \right]^{1/N}$$

The interpretation of this equation is, "The N-period spot rate is the geometric average of the current 1-year spot rate and the current $N-1$ forward rates ending at period N." For example, the 10-year spot rate should be the tenth root of the current spot multiplied by the following nine 1-year forward rates starting in one year.

Likewise, any 1-year rate must be readily determined by a combination of longer and shorter rates. The general expression for a 1-year forward rate in terms of the underlying spot rates is:

$$f_{N-1,N} = \frac{1+S_{0,N}}{1+S_{0,N-1}} - 1$$

The interpretation is, "The 1-year forward rate starting in $N-1$ years is the current N-period spot rate divided by the current $(N-1)$-year spot rate minus 1." The following equation calculates the implied 1-year forward rate starting in two years, $f_{2,1}$:

$$f_{2,1} = \frac{1+S_{0,3}}{1+S_{0,2}} - 1$$

In words, the 1-year forward rate starting in two years (i.e., the expected 1-year spot rate in two years) is the 3-year spot divided by the 2-year spot, minus 1.

©2011 Kaplan, Inc.

The Option-Adjusted Spread (OAS) and Zero-Volatility (Z) Spreads

The *nominal spread* is simply an issue's YTM minus the YTM of a Treasury security of similar maturity. Therefore, the use of the nominal spread suffers from the same limitations as the YTM.

The *static spread* (or *zero-volatility spread*) is not the spread over a single Treasury's YTM, but the spread over each of the spot rates on the spot rate yield curve. In other words, *the same spread is added to all risk-free spot rates* to make the PV of the bond's promised cash flows equal to its market price. The Z-spread is inherently more accurate than (and will usually differ from) the nominal spread, because it is based upon the arbitrage-free spot rates, rather than a given YTM. The Z-spread will equal the nominal spread if the term structure of interest rates (the yield curve) is perfectly flat.

The *option-adjusted spread* is used when a bond has embedded options. It can be thought of as the difference between the static or Z-spread and the option cost.

> Z-spread − option-adjusted spread = option cost in %

For a bond with a call feature, the option cost will be positive (you require a higher yield). For a bond with a put feature, the option cost will be negative because a bond with a put feature will have a lower required yield than an identical option-free bond.

The intuition of the OAS is that it is the spread once any differences in yield due to the embedded option are removed. Thus, it is a spread that reflects differences in yield for differences in credit risk and liquidity. That's why it must be used for bonds with embedded options and will be the same as the Z-spread for option-free bonds.

INTEREST RATE RISK

Duration is a measure of the *slope* of the price-yield function, which is steeper at low interest rates and flatter at high interest rates. Hence, duration (interest rate sensitivity) is higher at low rates and lower at high rates. This concept holds for noncallable bonds. Convexity is a measure of the degree of curvature of the price/yield relationship. Convexity accounts for the error in the estimated change in a bond's price based on duration.

Figure 9: Price-Yield Function of an Option-Free Bond

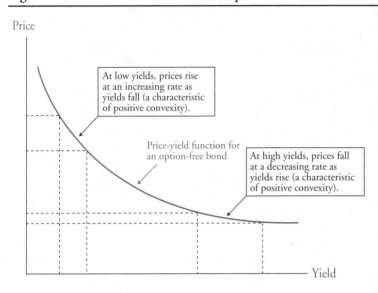

At low yields, prices rise at an increasing rate as yields fall (a characteristic of positive convexity).

Price-yield function for an option-free bond

At high yields, prices fall at a decreasing rate as yields rise (a characteristic of positive convexity).

If the bond is callable and the bond is likely to be called, as yields fall, no one will pay a price higher than the call price. The price will not rise significantly as yields fall and you will see *negative convexity* at work. Remember, the verbal description of negative convexity is, "As yields fall, prices rise at a decreasing rate." For a positively convex bond, as yields fall, prices rise at an *increasing* rate.

Figure 10: Price-Yield Function of a Callable Bond

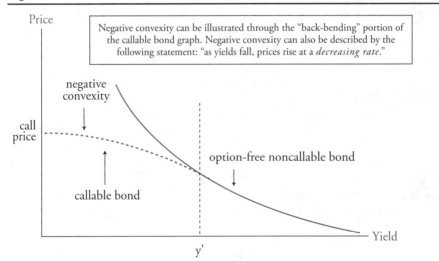

Negative convexity can be illustrated through the "back-bending" portion of the callable bond graph. Negative convexity can also be described by the following statement: "as yields fall, prices rise at a *decreasing rate*."

negative convexity

call price

option-free noncallable bond

callable bond

©2011 Kaplan, Inc.

Measuring Interest Rate Risk

There are two approaches to measuring interest rate risk: the full valuation approach (scenario analysis approach) and the duration/convexity approach.

Full valuation or scenario analysis approach:

This approach revalues all bonds in a portfolio under a given interest rate change (yield curve) scenario. It is theoretically preferred and gives a good idea of the change in portfolio value. This method requires accurate valuation models and consists of these steps:

Step 1: Start with current market yield and price.
Step 2: Estimate changes in yields.
Step 3: Revalue bonds.
Step 4: Compare new value to current value.

Duration/convexity approach:

This approach provides an approximation of the actual interest rate sensitivity of a bond or bond portfolio. It has an advantage due to its simplicity compared to the full valuation approach.

The most concise, useful description of duration is that it represents *the sensitivity of a bond's (or portfolio's) price to a 1% change in yield to maturity.*

Know this formula for effective duration and be able to make computations with this formula, entering Δy as a decimal (e.g., 0.005 for one-half percent):

$$\text{effective duration} = \frac{\text{value when yield falls by } \Delta y - \text{value when yield rises by } \Delta y}{2 \times \text{beginning value} \times (\Delta y)}$$

The preceding equation provides a measure that allows us to approximate the percentage change in the price of a bond for a 100 basis point (1%) change in yield to maturity.

Modified duration assumes that the cash flows on the bond will not change (i.e., that we are dealing with a noncallable bond). This differs from *effective duration*, which considers expected changes in cash flows that may occur for bonds with embedded options. Effective duration must be used for bonds with embedded options.

Level I and II Refresher

Modified duration and *effective duration* are good approximations of potential bond price behavior only for relatively small changes in interest rates. As rate changes grow larger, the curvature of the bond price/yield relationship becomes more important. The widening error in the estimated price is due to the curvature of the actual price path, *a bond's convexity.*

The *price value of a basis point* (PVBP) is the dollar change in a portfolio or asset value for one basis point change in yield.

$$\text{PVBP} = \text{duration} \times 0.0001 \times \text{value}$$

GENERAL PRINCIPLES OF CREDIT ANALYSIS

Credit Risk

Credit risk is comprised of the following three types of risk:

1. *Default risk* is the risk that the borrower will not repay the obligation.

2. *Credit spread risk* is the risk that the credit spread will increase and cause the value of the issue to decrease and/or cause the bond to underperform its benchmark.

3. *Downgrade risk* is the risk that the issue will be downgraded by the credit rating agencies, which will also cause the bond price to fall, and/or cause the bond to underperform its benchmark.

Credit ratings issued by the nationally recognized rating agencies (e.g., Standard & Poor's, Moody's, and Fitch) assess only default risk.

The Four Cs of Credit

1. *Character* refers to management's past dealings with bondholders and its ability to deal with unexpected events. An important focus of the analysis of the quality of management involves the firm's corporate governance structure. Studies have shown that companies with a greater degree of institutional ownership and stronger outside control of the board of directors have lower bond yields and higher credit ratings. Corporate governance is especially important for lower-rated corporate bonds because traditional credit analysis (ratio and cash flow analysis) may not be useful in assessing the issuer's ability to satisfy its future financial obligations.

©2011 Kaplan, Inc.

2. There are two kinds of *covenants*. Affirmative covenants specify things the firm must do, such as pay taxes, maintain working capital, and report results. Negative covenants specify things the firm cannot do, such as sell assets, pay dividends, or make additional borrowings.

3. *Collateral* includes the assets offered by the issuer as security to back the debt.

4. *Capacity* refers to the corporate borrower's ability to generate cash flow or liquidate short-term assets to repay its debt obligations.

Analysis of High-Yield Corporate Issuers

There are some special considerations for high-yield (i.e., junk) borrowers:

- **Corporate structure.** High-yield issuers are often structured as a holding company. It is necessary to analyze the cash flows of the subsidiaries, as well as how the cash shifts between the subsidiary companies and the parent company.
- **Debt structure.** High-yield issuers typically have *significant amounts* of *bank debt* on their balance sheet. The presence of bank loans in the debt structure of a high-yield issuer has three effects on the credit analysis of the high-yield issue: (1) because bank debt is *floating rate*, a cash flow analysis under different interest rate scenarios is necessary; (2) because bank debt is *short term*, the analyst must determine how and where funds will be obtained to pay off the bank debt that is about to mature; and (3) because bank debt is *senior*, it has a higher claim against the assets of the firm than debt that is carried on the books as *junior* debt.

Asset-Backed Securities Credit Analysis

Asset-backed debt is debt that is backed by a pool of loans or receivables (e.g., bonds backed by a pool of mortgages). In assessing the credit risk of asset-backed securities, analysts focus on four areas:

1. *Quality of the collateral.* This is extremely important for asset-backed securities (ABS) because the collateral is the source of repayment.

2. *Quality of the servicer.* The servicer is the entity that collects payments, handles defaults, and disburses payment to the bondholders.

3. *Cash flow stress and payment structure.* Not all tranches are paid the same way.

4. *Legal structure.* The legal structure affects how cash flow is distributed in the event of bankruptcy. The special purpose vehicle (SPV) is a legal entity that ensures that if the sponsor goes into bankruptcy, the collateral backing the asset-backed issue is not used to pay the general creditors of the sponsor.

Municipal Bond Credit Analysis

Municipal (muni) debt is issued by state and local governments. A key feature of muni debt is that the interest payments are not subject to federal income taxation. There are two kinds of muni debt:

1. *Tax-backed debt* relies on the tax revenues of the issuer for repayment. Tax-backed municipal bond analysis involves four factors: (1) issuer's debt structure, (2) budgetary policy, (3) local tax and intergovernmental revenue availability, and (4) issuer's socioeconomic environment.
2. *Revenue bonds* depend on the revenue from a specific project for repayment (e.g., revenues from a toll road). The risk of revenue bonds is dependent on (1) the adequacy of cash flows generated from the project being financed and (2) the reliability of bond covenants to ensure project revenues are not redirected for other purposes.

Sovereign Debt

Sovereign debt refers to the debt of national governments. Each national government (other than the U.S. government) is given two sovereign debt ratings: a *local currency rating* and a *foreign currency rating*.

When evaluating the credit of a national government, the key considerations are economic risk and political risk.

- *Economic risk* deals with the national government's ability to repay the debt. In assessing economic risk, rating agencies look at economic and income structure, economic growth prospects, and fiscal and monetary policy.
- *Political risk*, which deals with the willingness to pay, involves consideration of the form of government, the degree of political stability, the integration of the national economy into the world economy, and security risks.

Credit Analysis: Key Considerations

- The two most important factors in an analysis of a corporate issuer are the capacity to pay (particularly a cash flow analysis) and the corporate governance structure. This requires an analysis of the issuer's operational risk.
- ABS credit analysis requires an assessment of collateral credit quality, but analysis of business and operational risks is not important.
- Municipal bond credit analysis is very similar to corporate bond analysis, focusing on capacity to repay for both tax-backed and revenue bonds and willingness to repay (corporate character) for tax-backed bonds. The only important difference is that revenue bonds have rate covenants and a priority of revenue claims clause.
- Sovereign credit analysis requires an assessment of the country's ability to repay (economic risk) and willingness to repay (political risk).

 ©2011 Kaplan, Inc.

TERM STRUCTURE AND VOLATILITY OF INTEREST RATES

The Yield Curve

The *yield curve* is the relationship between interest rates and time to maturity. Think of the yield curve as the graphical representation of the *term structure of interest rates*. The yield curve takes one of three shapes: normal (upward-sloping), flat, or inverted (downward-sloping).

The yield curve can change in three ways:[2]

1. A *parallel shift* is when all maturities change by the same amount (e.g., if 1-year rates go up 2%, the 25-year rates also go up 2%). Parallel shifts explain 90% of the observed variation in total bond return variance.
2. A *nonparallel shift* (i.e., a twist) occurs when the slope of the yield curve either steepens or flattens. Nonparallel shifts explain about 8.5% of total bond return variance.
3. A *butterfly twist* refers to changes in the "humped" nature of the curve (i.e., the curve twists to become either more or less humped). These curvature changes only explain about 1.5% of total bond return variance.

Swap Rate Curve as Benchmark

The *swap rate curve* (a.k.a. the LIBOR curve) is the series of swap rates quoted by swap dealers over maturities extending from 2–30 years that reflects only the credit risk of the counterparty, which is usually a bank, so the swap curve is a AA-rated curve, not a default-free curve. The swap rate curve is preferred over a government bond yield curve for use as a benchmark.

Key Rate Duration

Key rate duration is the approximate percentage change in the value of a bond or bond portfolio in response to a 100 basis point change in a key rate, holding all other rates constant. In other words, you can determine the key rate duration for a portfolio by changing one spot rate (e.g., the 5-year rate) and observing the change in value of the portfolio. Keep in mind that every security or portfolio has a set of key rate durations, one for each key rate. Key rate duration is particularly useful for measuring the effect of a nonparallel shift in the yield curve on a bond portfolio because the overall portfolio effect is the sum of the individual effects.

---

2. Empirical results are reported in Robert Litterman and Jose Scheinkman, "Common Factors Affective Bond Returns," *Journal of Fixed Income* (June 1991), pp.54–61.

MORTGAGE-BACKED SECTOR OF THE BOND MARKET

A *mortgage-backed security* (MBS) is a bond with cash flows derived from a pool of mortgage loans (mortgage loans are loans used to finance the purchase of real estate). Most of the mortgage loans used as collateral for MBS are fixed-rate, fully amortizing loans. This means the payments from the mortgages don't change as interest rates change, and the payments include both principal and interest.

Prepayment Risk

The difficult feature of MBS valuation is that the underlying mortgages are subject to prepayment. This means the borrowers can prepay all or part of the principal value at any time. To a large extent, this *prepayment risk* is associated with interest rates (as interest rates fall, the borrowers tend to refinance their mortgage loans at lower rates, causing high prepayments on mortgages in the existing MBS pool).

The simplest type of MBS is a *passthrough security*. With a mortgage passthrough, all payments from the underlying mortgages (both principal and interest) are passed along to the security holders on a *pro rata* basis. The problem with valuing a passthrough is that there is great uncertainty about what the cash flow pattern will be because of prepayment risk.

The speed of prepayment will be influenced by three factors:
1. **Prevailing mortgage rates** affect prepayments by influencing the:
   - *Spread between the current mortgage rate and the original mortgage rate.* If a homeowner is holding a high-interest-rate mortgage and current mortgage rates fall, the incentive to refinance is large.
   - *Path of mortgage rates.* The path that mortgage rates follow on their way to the current level will affect prepayments today. The tendency for prepayments to drop when rates fall, rise, and fall again is called refinancing burnout.
2. **Housing turnover** increases as rates fall and housing becomes more affordable. Housing turnover is also higher when economic growth is higher.
3. Two particular **characteristics of the underlying mortgages** also affect the level of prepayments: seasoning (i.e., the age of the loan) and property location. Prepayments are low for new mortgages but increase as the loan seasons [the Public Securities Association (PSA) benchmark reflects this idea]. Local economics also influence prepayments, which tend to be faster in some parts of the country and slower in others.

Collateralized Mortgage Obligations (CMOs)

CMOs are securities issued against passthrough securities (i.e., securities secured by other securities) for which the cash flows have been reallocated to different

 ©2011 Kaplan, Inc.

bond classes called *tranches*, each having a different claim against the cash flows of the mortgage passthroughs or pool from which they were derived. Each CMO tranche represents a different mixture of contraction and extension risk. Hence, CMO securities can be more closely matched to the unique asset/liability needs of institutional investors and investment managers.

Commercial MBS

Commercial mortgage-backed securities (CMBS) are collateralized by a pool of commercial mortgage loans on income-producing properties, such as warehouses, office buildings, or apartments.

There are two important differences between residential MBS and CMBS:

1. Residential MBS loans are repaid by homeowners; CMBS loans are repaid by real estate investors who, in turn, rely on tenants and customers to provide the cash flow to repay the mortgage loan.
2. CMBS mortgages are structured as *non-recourse* loans, meaning the lender can only look to the collateral as means to repay the loan. The residential mortgage lender can go back to the borrower personally in an attempt to repay a delinquent mortgage loan.

For these reasons, the analysis of CMBS focuses on the credit risk of the property and not the borrower. CMBS structures focus on two key ratios to assess credit risk:

$$\text{debt-to-service coverage ratio} = \frac{\text{net operating income}}{\text{debt service}}$$

$$\text{loan-to-value ratio} = \frac{\text{current mortgage amount}}{\text{current appraised value}}$$

Loan-level call protection is created by a prepayment lockout, defeasance, prepayment penalty points, and yield maintenance charges. *CMBS-level call protection* is created by segregating pools into credit tranches.

ASSET-BACKED SECTOR OF THE BOND MARKET

Asset-backed securities (ABS) are backed by pools of loans or receivables other than primary mortgages. Some ABS are backed by amortizing loans (with scheduled principal payments), and others are backed by non-amortizing loans (with no scheduled principal payments). Because non-amortizing loans have no scheduled principal payments, they have no prepayment risk.

Basic Features of a Securitization Transaction

The key parties to a securitization transaction are the:

- Seller, who originates the loans and sells them to the issuer/trust.
- Issuer/trust, who buys the loans from the seller and issues the ABS.
- Servicer, who services the original loans.

See Figure 11 for an example of Fred Motor Company, which wants to remove $1 billion in auto loans from its balance sheet.

Figure 11: Structure of Fred Motor Company Asset Securitization

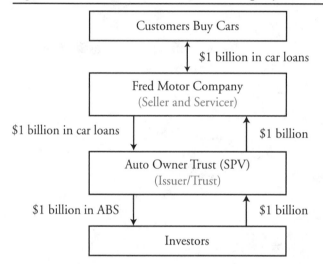

Types of ABS

There are several classes of assets that are used to create ABS. The most common are as follows:

- *Closed-end home equity loans* (HELs) are secondary mortgages structured just like a standard fixed-rate, fully amortizing mortgage. The pattern of prepayments from HELs differs from MBS prepayment patterns primarily because of differences in the credit traits of the borrowers. Therefore, analysts must consider the credit of the borrowers when analyzing HEL-backed securities. HEL floaters have a variable coupon rate cap called the available funds cap. HEL structures frequently include non-accelerating senior tranches and planned amortization class (PAC) tranches.

           ©2011 Kaplan, Inc.

- *Manufactured housing ABS* are backed by loans for manufactured homes. Prepayments for manufactured ABS are relatively stable because the underlying loans are not as sensitive to refinancing because:
  - Small loan balances reduce the extent of savings resulting from refinancing.
  - Initial depreciation of mobile homes may be such that the loan principal exceeds the asset value.
  - Borrowers often have relatively low credit ratings, making it difficult to refinance.
- *Auto loan-backed securities* are backed by loans for automobiles. Auto loans have 36- to 72-month maturities and are issued by the financial subsidiaries of auto manufacturers, commercial banks, credit unions, et cetera. Prepayments for auto loan-backed securities are caused by sales and trade-ins, the repossession/resale prices, insurance payoffs due to thefts and accidents, borrower payoffs, and refinancing. Refinancing is of minor importance, because many auto loans are frequently below market rates due to sales promotions.
- *Student loan ABS* are most often securitized by loans made under the U.S. government's Federal Family Education Loan Program (FFELP). Qualifying FFELP loans carry a U.S. government guarantee. Prepayments may occur because of defaults (inflows from the government guarantee process) or loan consolidation.
- *SBA (Small Business Administration) loan-backed securities* are backed by pools of SBA loans with similar terms and features. Most SBA loans are variable-rate loans, reset quarterly or monthly, and are based on the prime rate.
- *Credit-card receivables ABS* are backed by pools of receivables owed by banks, retailers, travel and entertainment companies, and other credit card issuers. The cash flow to a pool of credit card receivables includes finance charges, annual fees, and principal repayments. Credit cards have periodic payment schedules, but because their balances are revolving, the principal is not amortized. Because of this characteristic, interest on credit card ABS is paid periodically, but no principal is paid to the ABS holders during the lockout period, which may last from 18 months to 10 years.

Collateralized Debt Obligations

Collateralized debt obligations (CDOs) are collateralized by a pool of debt obligations comprised of one or more of the following assets: corporate bonds, MBS and ABS, bond issues in emerging markets, corporate loans advanced by commercial banks, and special situations and distressed debt.

The securities that back a cash CDO are cash market debt securities, such as corporate bonds, previously described. Cash CDOs can be arbitrage driven, in which the motivation is to generate an arbitrage return on the spread between return on the collateral and the funding costs, or balance sheet driven, in which the motivation is to remove assets (and the associated funding) from the balance sheet.

In a *synthetic CDO*, the bondholders take on the economic risks of the underlying assets but do not take legal ownership of them. This is accomplished by linking certain contingent payments to a reference asset (e.g., a bond index). There are three advantages to a synthetic CDO versus a cash CDO:

1. The senior section doesn't require funding.
2. The ramp-up period is shorter.
3. It's cheaper to acquire an exposure to the reference asset through the credit default swap instead of buying the asset directly.

 ©2011 Kaplan, Inc.

PORTFOLIO MANAGEMENT

A risk-averse investor prefers higher to lower expected returns for the same level of expected risk and prefers lower to higher risk for a given level of expected returns. There is a positive relationship between expected returns and risk.

Return Objectives

Capital preservation. Earning a return at least equal to the inflation rate.

Capital appreciation. Earning a *nominal* return that exceeds the inflation rate. Purchasing power of the initial investment increases over time through capital gains.

Current income. Investments with dividend and/or interest income, generally to pay living expenses or some other planned spending need.

Total return. Objective of having a portfolio grow in value to meet a future need through both capital gains and the reinvestment of current portfolio income.

Expected Return

Expected rate of return from *expectational* data (a probability model) for a risky asset is a weighted average of the rates of return, where the weights are the probabilities of occurrence for each rate of return.

$$\hat{R} = \sum_{i=1}^{n}(P_i R_i) = P_1 R_1 + P_2 R_2 + \ldots + P_n R_n$$

where:
P_i = probability that state i will occur
R_i = asset return if the economy is in state i

Variance and Standard Deviation

Variance of the rate of return for a risky asset calculated from expectational data (a probability model) is the probability-weighted sum of the squared differences between the returns in each state and the overall expected return.

$$\text{expected variance} = \hat{\sigma}^2 = \sum_{i=1}^{n}\left\{ [R_i - \hat{R}_i]^2 \times P_i \right\}$$

$$\text{expected standard deviation} = \hat{\sigma} = \sqrt{\hat{\sigma}^2}$$

Covariance and Correlation

Covariance measures the extent to which two variables move together over time. The covariance is an absolute measure of movement and is measured in return units squared.

Using *historical data*, we multiply each variable's deviation from its mean by the other variable's deviation from its mean for each period, add them all up, and divide by the number of (paired) observations.

$$cov_{1,2} = \frac{\sum_{t=1}^{n} \{[R_{t,1} - \overline{R}_1][R_{t,2} - \overline{R}_2]\}}{n-1}$$

With *expectational data* (a probability model), we multiply the differences between each variable and its expected value for each possible outcome (state) together and take the weighted sum, where the weights are the probabilities of each particular outcome or state (e.g., good market, average market, and poor market).

$$\text{expected } cov_{1,2} = \sum_{i=1}^{n} \left\{ P_i \left[R_{i,1} - \hat{R}_1 \right] \left[R_{i,2} - \hat{R}_2 \right] \right\}$$

Covariance can be standardized by dividing by the product of the standard deviations of the two securities. This standardized measure of co-movement is called their *correlation coefficient* and is computed as:

$$\text{correlation of assets 1 and 2} = \rho_{1,2} = \frac{cov_{1,2}}{\sigma_1 \sigma_2} \text{ so that } cov_{1,2} = \rho_{1,2} \sigma_1 \sigma_2$$

Risk and Return for a Portfolio of Risky Assets

When risky assets are combined into a portfolio, the expected portfolio return is a weighted average of the asset returns, where the weights are the percentages of the total portfolio value invested in each asset.

The standard deviation of returns for a portfolio of risky assets depends on the standard deviations of each asset's return (σ), the proportion of the portfolio in each asset (w), and, crucially, on the covariance or correlation of returns between each asset pair in the portfolio.

©2011 Kaplan, Inc.

Portfolio standard deviation for a 2-asset portfolio:

$$\sigma_p = \sqrt{w_1^2\sigma_1^2 + w_2^2\sigma_2^2 + 2w_1w_2\sigma_1\sigma_2\rho_{1,2}}$$

which is equivalent to:

$$\sigma_p = \sqrt{w_1^2\sigma_1^2 + w_2^2\sigma_2^2 + 2w_1w_2cov_{1,2}}$$

Efficient Frontier

The Markowitz efficient frontier represents the set of portfolios that have the highest expected return for a given level of risk and the least risk for a given level of expected return, where risk is measured as standard deviation of returns.

An individual investor's optimal (most preferred) portfolio is the risk return combination represented by the point on the efficient frontier that lies on the investor's highest (most preferred) indifference curve. As shown in the following figure, a more risk-averse investor will choose a point like X, compared to a less risk-averse investor who will choose a riskier portfolio, such as Y.

Figure 12: Locating the Optimal Portfolio

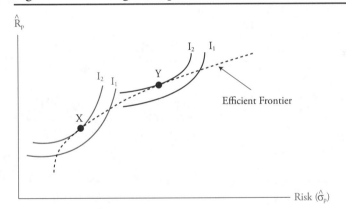

ASSET PRICING MODELS

Assumptions of Capital Market Theory

- All investors use the Markowitz mean-variance framework to select securities and, therefore, select only portfolios that lie on the efficient frontier.
- There is unlimited lending and borrowing at the risk-free rate.
- Investors have identical expectations.
- There is a 1-period horizon.

- Divisible assets—all assets are infinitely divisible.
- Markets are frictionless—no taxes or transaction costs.
- There is no inflation (or perfectly anticipated inflation).
- Interest rates are constant.
- Capital markets are in equilibrium.

When a risk-free asset is combined with a risky asset in a portfolio, varying the proportions of the two assets results in a set of risk-return combinations that lie on a straight line. The following figure illustrates the possible risk-return combinations from combining a risk-free asset with three different (efficient) portfolios, X, Y, and M.

Figure 13: Combining a Risk-Free Asset With a Risky Portfolio

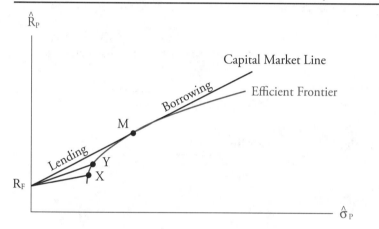

This figure also illustrates the point that combining a risk-free asset with risky Portfolio M (the *tangency* portfolio) results in the best available combination of risk and return. Combining the risk-free asset with either risky Portfolio X or risky Portfolio Y results in a less-preferred set of possible portfolios.

Because investors who hold risky assets will choose to hold Portfolio M, it must contain *all* available risky assets, and we can describe it as the *market portfolio*.

Investors at Point M have 100% of their funds invested in Portfolio M. Between R_f and M, investors hold both the risk-free asset and Portfolio M. This means investors are *lending* some of their funds at the risk-free rate and investing the rest in the risky market Portfolio M. To the right of M, investors hold more than 100% of Portfolio M. This means they are *borrowing* funds to buy more of Portfolio M. The *levered positions* represent a 100% investment in Portfolio M and borrowing to invest even more in Portfolio M.

In short, adding a risk-free asset to the set of risky assets considered in the Markowitz portfolio theory results in a new efficient frontier that is now a straight line, the capital market line (CML).

©2011 Kaplan, Inc.

Security Market Line: Systematic and Unsystematic Risk

Under the assumptions of capital market theory, diversification is costless, and investors will only hold efficient portfolios. The risk that is eliminated by diversification is called *unsystematic risk* (also referred to as unique, diversifiable, or firm-specific risk). Because unsystematic risk can be eliminated at no cost, investors need not be compensated in equilibrium for bearing unsystematic risk.

The risk that remains in efficient portfolios is termed *systematic risk* (also referred to as non-diversifiable or market risk), which is measured by an asset's or portfolio's beta. Therefore, we conclude that only systematic or market risk requires additional expected returns in equilibrium. This crucial result is the basis for the capital asset pricing model (CAPM). The equilibrium relationship between systematic risk and expected return is illustrated by the security market line (SML).

The *total risk* (standard deviation of returns) for any asset or portfolio of assets can be separated into systematic and unsystematic risk.

> total risk = systematic risk + unsystematic risk

Well-diversified (efficient) portfolios have no unsystematic risk, and a risk-free asset has no systematic (market) risk either. Systematic risk is measured in units of market risk referred to as the beta of an asset or portfolio, so that the beta of the market portfolio is equal to one. The market portfolio simply has one "unit" of market risk.

Figure 14: Security Market Line

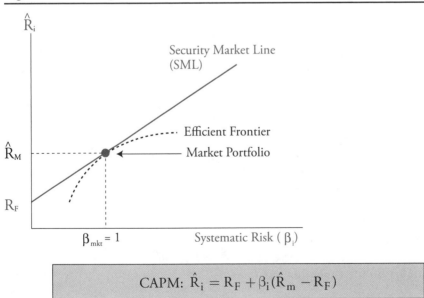

$$\text{CAPM:} \quad \hat{R}_i = R_F + \beta_i (\hat{R}_m - R_F)$$

Note that required return and expected return are the same in equilibrium.

SML and Equilibrium

You should be able to compute expected return using the SML and state whether a security is underpriced or overpriced relative to its equilibrium value. In solving problems, be careful to note whether you are given the expected return on the market, $\hat{R}_M$, or the market risk premium, $\hat{R}_M - R_F$.

An analyst may identify assets for which his forecasted returns differ from the expected return based on the asset's beta. Assets for which the expected return differs from equilibrium expected returns will plot either above or below the SML. Consider three stocks, A, B, and C, that are plotted on the SML based on their forecasted returns:

Figure 15: Identifying Mispriced Securities

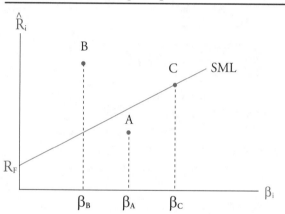

Asset B plots above the SML, so it is underpriced. The interpretation is that the forecasted return is greater than the return necessary to compensate for the asset's systematic risk in equilibrium. A higher-than-equilibrium return implies a lower-than-equilibrium price. Asset A is *overpriced*, by the same reasoning, and Asset C is priced at its equilibrium value.

Relaxing the Assumptions of the CAPM

- With *different borrowing and lending rates*, we cannot derive a security's systematic risk. However, the CAPM remains valid if we introduce a *zero-beta portfolio* that has returns uncorrelated with the market return.
- *The addition of transactions costs, heterogeneous expectations,* or *different planning periods* turn the SML from a line to a band.
- Allowing for *taxes* creates different SMLs and CMLs for investors, depending on their marginal tax rates.

 ©2011 Kaplan, Inc.

THE CAPITAL ALLOCATION LINE AND THE CAPITAL MARKET LINE

In Figure 16, the return on T-bills is shown on the y-axis at 6% (6% return and zero standard deviation). Any combination of the risk-free asset and a risky portfolio with positive weights will fall on a straight line between the two.

Figure 16: Capital Allocation Line

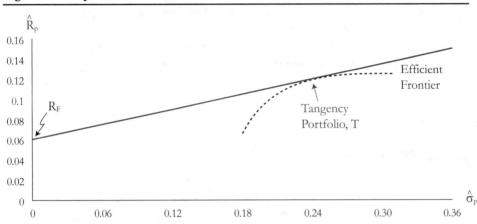

The **capital allocation line** (CAL) is the line from the risk-free rate to the point of tangency on the efficient frontier. When a risk-free asset is available, all investors are better off selecting a portfolio that falls on the CAL. The CAL in effect becomes the new efficient frontier.

The point of tangency between the CAL and the efficient frontier represents the **best risky portfolio** because when it is combined with a risk-free asset, it is optimal in the sense that it has the highest possible reward-to-risk ratio:

$$\frac{\hat{R}_T - R_F}{\sigma_T}$$

The reward-to-risk ratio can also be viewed as the expected risk premium $\hat{R}_T - R_F$ for each unit of risk, σ_T, and is the Sharpe ratio for Portfolio T.

The CAL equation:

$$\hat{R}_P = R_F + \left(\frac{\hat{R}_M - R_F}{\sigma_M}\right)\sigma_P$$

Here's what you need to remember about the CAL:

- If a risk-free investment is available, investors can combine it with a risky portfolio to increase their return at all levels of risk.

- The CAL is the straight line that intersects the y-axis at the risk-free rate and lies tangent to the efficient frontier.
- The intercept of the CAL equals the risk-free rate, and the slope equals the maximum portfolio reward-to-risk ratio, defined as $[\hat{R}_T - R_F] / \sigma_T$.
- The tangency portfolio is the optimal risky portfolio because it has the highest possible expected reward-to-risk tradeoff.
- The CAL can be used to determine the risk associated with any desired target return or the expected return associated with any desired target standard deviation that falls on the CAL.
- The intercept and slope of the CAL depend on the asset expectations of the investor. Therefore, investors with different asset expectations will face different CALs.

If the market portfolio (*M*) is the tangency portfolio, the CML equation becomes:

$$\hat{R}_P = R_F + \left(\frac{\hat{R}_M - R_F}{\sigma_M}\right)\sigma_P$$

The key conclusion of the CML is that all investors will make optimal investment decisions by allocating between the risk-free asset and the market portfolio.

Differences Between the CAL and the CML

Although the CAL and CML are generated using exactly the same mean-variance calculations, there are a few important differences:

- There is only one CML because it is developed assuming all investors agree on the expected return, standard deviation, and correlations for all assets.
- There is an unlimited number of CALs because each is developed uniquely for each investor.
- The tangency portfolio for the CML is the *market* portfolio, and there is only one market portfolio. The market portfolio uses market value weights.
- The tangency portfolio for the CAL can differ across investors depending on differences in investor expectations.
- The CML is a special case of the CAL.

CAPM

The **CAPM** calculates the expected return for an asset based on its level of systematic (market-related) risk.

The CAPM equation (also referred to as the SML):

$$\hat{R}_i = R_F + \beta_i(\hat{R}_m - R_F)$$

©2011 Kaplan, Inc.

Figure 17: Key Differences Between the SML and the CML

	SML	CML
Measure of risk	Uses systematic risk beta (non-diversifiable risk).	Uses standard deviation (total risk).
Application	Tool used to determine the appropriate expected (benchmark) returns for securities.	Tool used to determine the appropriate asset allocation (percentages allocated to the risk-free asset and to the market portfolio) for the investor.
Definition	Graph of the capital asset pricing model.	Graph of the efficient frontier.
Slope	Market risk premium.	Market portfolio Sharpe ratio.

Beta is a measure of an asset's systematic risk:

$$beta_i = \frac{cov(i, M)}{\sigma_M^2} = \frac{\rho_{i,M}\sigma_i\sigma_M}{\sigma_M^2} = \frac{\sigma_i}{\sigma_M}\rho_{i,M}$$

The ex-post **market model** is the regression model often used to estimate betas for common stocks. Specifically, it defines the return to Asset i, R_i as:

$$R_i = \alpha_i + \beta_i R_M + \varepsilon_i$$

The market model makes three predictions:

$$1. \quad \hat{R}_i = \alpha_i + \beta_i \hat{R}_M$$

$$2. \quad \sigma_i^2 = \beta_i^2 \sigma_M^2 + \sigma_{\varepsilon_i}^2$$

$$3. \quad cov_{ij} = \beta_i \beta_j \sigma_M^2$$

Adjusted Beta

Historical betas may be very poor predictors of future betas. The beta instability problem is addressed by adjusting the beta to account for its tendency to gravitate to a value of 1 over time.

The general form of the *adjusted beta* equation can be presented as:

$$\text{forecast } \beta_{i,t} = \alpha_0 + \alpha_1 \beta_{i,t-1}$$

where:

sum of $\alpha_0 + \alpha_1$ is set equal to 1

The most popular values of α_0 and α_1 are $\alpha_0 = 1/3$ and $\alpha_1 = 2/3$.

MULTIFACTOR MODELS

1. *Macroeconomic factor models* use unexpected changes (surprises) in macroeconomic variables to explain asset returns.
2. *Fundamental factor models* use unexpected changes in microeconomic factors.
3. *Statistical factor models* determine which factors best explain returns on a cross section of securities.

The following model is an example of a 2-factor macroeconomic model in which stock returns are a function of unexpected changes in inflation and GDP:

$$R_i = a_i + b_{i1}F_{INF} + b_{i2}F_{GDP} + \varepsilon_i$$

The Macroeconomic Factor Model vs. the Fundamental Factor Model

The key differences between the macroeconomic factor model and the fundamental factor model can be summarized as follows:

- *Sensitivities.* The standardized sensitivities in the fundamental factor model (b_{i1} and b_{i2}) are calculated directly from the attribute (e.g., P/E) data—they are not estimated. This contrasts with the macroeconomic factor model, in which the sensitivities are regression slope estimates.
- *Interpretation of factors.* The macroeconomic factors (F_{GDP} and F_{QS}) are surprises in the macroeconomic variables (e.g., inflation shock and interest rate shock). In contrast, the fundamental factors ($F_{P/E}$ and F_{SIZE}) are rates of return associated with each factor and are estimated using multiple regression.
- *Number of factors.* Macroeconomic factors are intended to represent systematic risk factors and are usually small in number (parsimonious model). Fundamental factors often are large in number, providing a more cumbersome, yet more detailed, model of the risk-return relationship for assets.
- *Intercept term.* The intercept in the macroeconomic factor model equals the stock's expected return (based on market consensus expectations of the macro factors) from an equilibrium pricing model like the APT. In contrast, the intercept of a fundamental factor model with standardized sensitivities

©2011 Kaplan, Inc.

has no economic interpretation; it is simply the regression intercept necessary to make the unsystematic risk of the asset equal to zero.

APT and Other Factor Models

The **arbitrage pricing theory** (APT) model is an equilibrium asset-pricing model, like the CAPM, except that it makes less restrictive assumptions.

A k-factor model shows that the expected return on a diversified portfolio is linearly related to the factor sensitivities of that portfolio:

$$\hat{R}_p = R_F + \lambda_1 \beta_{p,1} + \ldots + \lambda_k \beta_{p,k}$$

- The APT is an equilibrium-pricing model, while macroeconomic multifactor models are *ad hoc*.
- The intercept term in a macroeconomic factor model is the asset's expected return, while the APT intercept is the risk-free rate.
- In general multifactor models, the factors represent surprises. In the APT, because it is an equilibrium model, the factors are actual risk premiums analogous to the market risk premium in the SML.

ACTIVE RISK AND RETURN

Active return is the difference between portfolio and benchmark returns $(R_P - R_B)$, and active risk is the standard deviation of active return over time. Active risk is determined by the manager's active factor tilt and active asset selection decisions:

active risk squared = active factor risk + active specific risk

Information Ratio

The information ratio is active return divided by active risk:

$$IR = \frac{\bar{R}_P - \bar{R}_B}{\sigma_{(R_P - R_B)}}$$

USES OF FACTOR AND TRACKING PORTFOLIOS

- A *factor portfolio* is exposed to only one factor.
- A *tracking portfolio* is constructed to have the same factor exposures as a benchmark. The manager generates alpha through security selection.

INTERNATIONAL ASSET PRICING

Integrated world markets are markets where capital can flow freely across borders, allowing investors to seek the most efficient portfolios. If capital flows freely, then securities with similar risk/return characteristics will be priced similarly in all markets relative to the world index. We would expect international markets to be reasonably integrated because there are a number of participants who have the ability to move capital between markets: institutional investors, multinational corporations, and governments.

However, if world markets are *segmented*, then impediments to the flow of capital prevent investors from taking advantage of relative mispricing between countries. In this case, the price of similar securities will not be the same in all markets. There are six potential impediments to the international flow of capital:

1. Psychological barriers.
2. Legal restrictions.
3. Transaction costs.
4. Discriminatory taxation.
5. Political risks.
6. Foreign currency risk.

Real Exchange Rate Risk

Professor's Note: In this section and throughout the Level III curriculum, the spot rate (S) is quoted in terms of domestic currency (DC) per unit of foreign currency (FC).

Real exchange rate risk is the possibility of changes in the nominal exchange rate that are not explained by changes in the price level. To determine whether the real exchange rate has changed, you can calculate the real exchange rate at two points in time. If the real exchange rate is the same at both points in time, any change in the nominal exchange rate is completely explained by inflation:

$$\text{real } S = \text{nominal } S \times \left(\frac{\text{FC price level}}{\text{DC price level}} \right)$$

S is quoted in DC/FC.

Real exchange rate movements are defined as changes in the nominal exchange rate that are not explained by inflation differentials:

% Δ in real S = % Δ in nominal S − [inflation (DC) − inflation (FC)]

where:
S = spot rate (in DC/FC)

©2011 Kaplan, Inc.

Foreign Currency Risk Premium

In addition to the normal sensitivity of asset returns to changes in the market, an international investor must also assess the *foreign currency risk premium* (FCRP) associated with each foreign currency:

$$FCRP = \frac{\hat{S}_1 - S_0}{S_0} - (r_{DC} - r_{FC})$$

Remember, S is quoted in DC/FC.

If interest rate parity holds, then:

$$FCRP = \frac{\hat{S}_1 - F}{S_0}$$

There are two ways to calculate the domestic currency (DC) return to holding a foreign bond:

1. DC return = interest rate (FC) + FC appreciation
2. DC return = interest rate (DC) + FCRP

International CAPM (ICAPM)

In an ICAPM world, all investors will hold some combination of their own country's risk-free asset and the world market portfolio (optimally hedged). The ICAPM pricing relationship accounts for an asset's sensitivity to changes in the world market portfolio and for the asset's sensitivity to changes in all world currencies:

$$\hat{R}_i = R_F + \left(\beta_g \times MRP_g\right) + \left(\gamma_1 \times FCRP_1\right) + \left(\gamma_2 \times FCRP_2\right) + ... + \left(\gamma_k \times FCRP_k\right)$$

where:

$\hat{R}_i$	= asset's expected return
R_F	= domestic currency risk-free rate
β_g	= sensitivity of the asset's domestic currency returns to changes in the global market portfolio
MRP_g	= world market risk premium $[\hat{R}_M - R_F]$
$\hat{R}_M$	= expected return on world market portfolio
γ_1 to γ_k	= sensitivities of asset's domestic currency returns to changes in the value of currencies 1 through k
$FCRP_{1\ to\ k}$	= foreign currency risk premiums on currencies 1 through k

ACTIVE PORTFOLIO MANAGEMENT

Active portfolio management refers to decisions of the portfolio manager to actively manage and monitor the broad asset allocation and security selection of the portfolio. The theory of active portfolio management can be justified:

- *Economically.* In an efficient market, investors will allocate funds to passively managed (indexed) portfolios. But as less money is actively managed, asset prices may begin to deviate from fair values, which, in turn, will attract transfers of cash flows into actively managed funds.
- *Empirically.* Some portfolio managers have demonstrated abnormally strong performance over extended periods. Consequently, investors seek actively managed funds that they think will be among the star performers.

THE INVESTMENT POLICY STATEMENT

Steps of the Portfolio Management Process

There are three steps of the portfolio management process: (1) planning, (2) execution, and (3) feedback. The *components of the planning phase* include:

- Analyzing objectives and constraints.
- Developing an investment policy statement.
- Determining the appropriate investment strategy.
- Selecting an appropriate asset allocation.

Investment Objectives

Risk objectives are those factors associated with an investor's willingness and ability to take risk. Combining willingness and ability to accept risk is termed *risk tolerance*. Risk aversion indicates an investor's inability and unwillingness to take risk.

Willingness to tolerate risk is determined by psychological factors (i.e., subjective factors). For example, some individuals might feel their portfolio is large or that they are better than others at interpreting market or firm information. Other people are just naturally "risk takers." When a client makes statements about risk tolerance, you should interpret the statements as indicators of willingness, not ability, to tolerate risk. Always consider what the client does.

The client's *ability to tolerate risk* is jointly determined by the size of the portfolio (not the client's perception of the size of the portfolio), the client's time horizon, and the client's spending (i.e., liquidity) needs.

 ©2011 Kaplan, Inc.

Guidelines on ability to tolerate risk:

- As the size of the portfolio increases → ability increases (*positive* relationship).
- As the time horizon increases → ability increases (*positive* relationship).
- As liquidity needs increase → ability decreases (*negative* relationship).

In deciding both the individual's willingness and ability, start the individual at *average* and then look for reasons to increase or lower.

Guidance on determining overall risk tolerance:

1. If willingness > ability → honor ability → recommend counseling to reconcile the difference.
2. If willingness < ability → honor willingness → recommend counseling to reconcile the difference.
3. If willingness < ability *and* the client is extremely wealthy → *average* the two and recommend counseling to reconcile the difference.

Return objectives are classed as either desired return (as stated by the client) or required return (as determined by financial obligations). Return objectives should be consistent with the investor's risk objectives. The objectives should differentiate between real and nominal returns, and pre-tax and after-tax returns. The return objective should be considered from a *total return perspective* reflecting both income and capital gains.

Investment Constraints

Liquidity constraints relate to expected or unexpected cash flows needed in the future. The liquidity constraint is closely linked to the risk and return objectives because liquidity needs will influence the ability to take risk and reduce expected return objectives.

Time horizon constraints are associated with the time period(s) during which the portfolio is expected to generate returns. There is also a link between time horizon constraints and risk objectives: long time horizons increase the investor's ability to take risk (although not necessarily the willingness to take risk).

Tax constraints are important for individual investors because return objectives are stated in after-tax terms.

Legal and regulatory constraints mainly affect institutional investors. The Prudent Investor Rule is an example of a legal constraint facing trustees.

The investor's *unique circumstances* also impose constraints.

ALTERNATIVE INVESTMENTS

 Professor's Note: Real estate, which is contained within Alternative Investments in the CFA curriculum, is also discussed in the Refresher section on Equity Valuation.

Alternative Investment Features and Characteristics

In the alternative investments material, you should become familiar with the basic characteristics of:

- Open-end and closed-end mutual funds.
- Exchange-traded funds (ETFs).
- Real estate.
- Venture capital.
- Hedge funds.
- Closely held companies.
- Commodities.

Open-End and Closed-End Funds

The *net asset value* (NAV) of an investment company (mutual fund) is the investment company's assets minus its liabilities, stated on a per-share basis.

An open-end investment company, or *open-end fund*, stands ready to redeem shares at any time during regular market hours, typically at the end-of-day NAV. Shares of a closed-end company, or *closed-end fund*, are traded after issuance in the secondary markets. Thus, the liquidity of an open-end fund is provided by the investment company that manages it, whereas the liquidity of a closed-end fund is provided by securities markets.

The managers of an *open-end fund* may charge a fee, or *load*, to the investors upon purchase (a front-end load) or at redemption (a back-end load). A fund that charges no fee at purchase or redemption is called a *no-load* fund. All funds, regardless of whether a load or no-load fund, will charge ongoing fees on an annual basis, which may include management fees, administrative fees, and marketing fees.

The shares of a *closed-end fund* will be issued at a small premium to the value of the underlying assets, the premium serving as compensation for issuance costs. The investment company will also charge an ongoing management fee. Because a closed-end fund is traded in the secondary market subsequent to issuance, the redemption cost for the investor is simply the bid/ask spread of the shares and the commission on the trade. Closed-end funds may trade at significant discounts or premiums to NAV.

 ©2011 Kaplan, Inc.

Exchange-Traded Funds

An *exchange-traded fund* (ETF) is a special type of fund that invests in a portfolio of stocks or bonds and is typically designed to mimic the performance of a specified index.

A feature unique to ETFs is their use of "in-kind" creation and redemption of shares. *Authorized participants* can exchange portfolios of stocks matching the ETF composition for newly created ETF shares or exchange ETF shares for an equivalent portfolio of the underlying stocks. This mechanism prevents the types of market discounts and premiums to NAV common with closed-end funds.

Advantages of ETFs:

- ETFs provide an efficient method of diversification.
- ETFs trade like stocks—they can be margined and shorted.
- Some ETFs may be patterned after indices that have active futures and option markets, allowing for better risk management.
- ETF investors know the exact composition of the fund at all times.
- ETFs typically have very efficient operating expense ratios, as well as no loads to purchase or redeem shares.
- ETFs may produce less capital gains tax liability.

Disadvantages of ETFs:

- In some countries outside of the United States, there are fewer indices for ETFs to track, resulting in mid- or low-cap stocks not being well-represented in the portfolio.
- The ability to trade ETFs intraday may not be significant to those investors with longer time horizons.
- Investors may encounter inefficient markets (large bid-ask spreads) in ETFs with low trading volume.
- Larger investors may choose to directly invest in an index portfolio, resulting in lower expenses and lower tax consequences.

Types of Real Estate Investments

- *Outright ownership.*
- *Leveraged equity position.*
- *Mortgages.*
- *Aggregation vehicles.* Common forms include real estate limited partnerships, commingled funds, and real estate investment trusts (REITs).

Characteristics of Real Estate Investments

Because each property is unique, it is impossible to directly compare to other properties, making it difficult to determine true market value. Real estate as an asset class is somewhat illiquid because it is immobile, indivisible, and difficult to value.

Common methods to value real estate:

- The *cost method* is determined by the replacement cost of improvements, plus an estimate for the value of the land. The market value of an existing property may differ significantly from its replacement cost.
- The *sales comparison method* uses the price of a similar property or properties from recent transactions. Prices from other properties must be adjusted for changes in market conditions and for characteristics unique to each property. In *hedonic* price estimation, sales prices are modeled as a linear function of key property characteristics related to value, and then the model coefficients are used with characteristic values for the subject property to estimate its value.
- The *income method* uses the discounted annual cash flow as if it were a perpetuity to calculate the present value of the future income stream produced by the property. The net operating income (NOI) is a simplified estimate of annual cash flow equal to annual potential gross rental income minus operating expenses, which includes an estimate of the percentage losses from vacancy and collection losses. The NOI is then divided by an estimate of the market-required rate of return on similar properties, resulting in an appraisal price.

This simplified model is used quite frequently.

$$\text{NOI} = \text{potential income } (1 - \text{vacancy and bad debt \%})$$
$$- \text{RE taxes} - \text{maintenance} - \text{other expenses}$$

$$\text{real estate value (income method)} = \frac{\text{NOI}}{\text{required return}}$$

- The *discounted after-tax cash flow model* is based on the cash flows to a specific investor and, therefore, depends on the investor's marginal tax rate and the assumed financing for the transaction. The net present value of the property is calculated as the present value of the annual after-tax cash flows, discounted at the investor's required rate of return, minus the initial cash investment. In calculating the annual after-tax operating cash flows, note that interest is tax deductible and principal repayments are not.

$$\text{annual after-tax operating cash flow} = (\text{NOI} - \text{depreciation} - \text{interest}) \times$$
$$(1 - \text{tax rate}) - \text{principal repayment}$$
$$+ \text{depreciation}$$

In the year of sale, the after-tax proceeds of the sale are added to that year's after-tax operating cash flows. Taxes (at the capital gains tax rate, on the difference

©2011 Kaplan, Inc.

between the depreciated property value and the sales price) and the remaining principal mortgage balance are subtracted from the sales price.

after-tax sale proceeds = sales price − mortgage balance − tax on gain

tax on gain = capital gains tax rate [sales price − (purchase price − depreciation)]

Venture Capital

Stages in venture capital investing:

- *Seed stage.* Investors are providing capital in the earliest stage of the business and may help fund research and development of product ideas.
- *Early stage.* Companies are entering operation phase but have yet to produce a market-ready product.
- *Formative stage.* Broad category that encompasses the seed stage and early stage.
- *Later stage.* Marketable goods are in production and sales efforts are underway, but the company is still privately held.

Within the *later stage*:

- *Second-stage investing* describes investments in a company that is producing and selling a product but is not yet generating income.
- *Third-stage financing* would fund a major expansion of the company.
- *Mezzanine* or *bridge financing* would enable a company to take the steps necessary to go public.

Hedge Funds: Leverage, Risk, and Survivorship Bias

Historically, hedge funds actually hedged risk. Currently, the term is used for many investment strategies that have the form of a private partnership, are largely unregulated, and have an incentive performance fee structure. Many hedge funds have concentrated investments (low diversification) and utilize some type of leverage.

The net return of a hedge fund is calculated by subtracting all manager fees from its gross performance.

Risks associated with hedge funds include the following:

- Illiquidity.
- Potential for mispricing.
- Counterparty credit risk.
- Settlement errors.
- Short covering.
- Margin calls.

Compared to other asset classes, hedge funds tend to have higher returns, lower standard deviation of returns, and higher Sharpe ratios. There are, however, certain biases in reported performance and a smoothing due to value estimation of non-traded assets.

The effect of *survivorship bias* from not reporting the results of failed funds is greater for a hedge fund database than for other asset classes because of the lack of required reporting standards in the industry.

Fund managers tend to "cherry pick" the information they choose to release, reporting on their more successful funds while not providing information on poorly performing funds. Reported returns for a hedge fund database are therefore overstating performance because of both survivorship bias and cherry picking.

Survivorship bias has the opposite effect on the risk measures of a hedge fund database. Hedge funds with highly volatile returns tend to fail more frequently, and defunct funds are not generally included in the database. Because the database would only include the more stable funds that have survived, the risk measure of hedge funds as an asset class would be understated.

In a *fund of funds* hedge fund, a manager selects a number of hedge funds, and investors purchase interests in the overall fund.

Advantages include diversification and risk reduction, professional selection of included funds, and possible access to closed funds.

Disadvantages are higher fees and the possibility that fund selection will be poor.

Closely Held Company Valuation

There are three primary valuation methods:

1. The *cost approach*. The cost to replace the firm's assets.
2. The *comparables approach*. Value relative to that of a benchmark company.
3. The *income approach*. The present value of the expected future cash flows.

Valuation discounts to the valuations of publicly traded companies are used to adjust for lack of liquidity, lack of marketability, and lack of control when valuing a minority interest.

A control premium is appropriate when valuing a controlling interest in a privately held company.

 ©2011 Kaplan, Inc.

Commodity Investing

Investing in commodities tends to hedge investments in companies that use those same commodities in production. Most investors do not choose to invest in commodities directly, but rather through the purchase of futures contracts, bonds indexed to a commodity price, or the equity of commodity-producing companies.

Futures contracts are usually the most efficient way to participate in the commodities market, but the common stock of commodity producers can also be an effective way to gain exposure to increasing production and consumption in the economy.

Establishing a collateralized commodity futures position involves simultaneously purchasing futures contracts and an amount of government securities equal to the value of the entire futures position. The total return on this strategy will equal the change in price of the futures contract plus the interest earned on the government securities.

Derivatives

Derivative Markets and Instruments

A *derivative* is a security that *derives* its value from the value of, or return on, another asset or security.

A *contingent claim* has a payoff in the future only if certain events happen. Option contracts are contingent claims and also derivative securities.

A *forward commitment* is just that: a contractual commitment to buy or sell an asset in the future or take or make a loan in the future. Futures, swaps, and forward contracts are forward commitments and are also derivative securities.

Forwards and swaps are typically originated by dealers and have no active secondary market. Futures contracts are originated by and traded in a futures exchange. Some options contracts are traded on an organized options exchange and others are originated by dealers and do not trade in a secondary market.

Overview of Derivative Contracts

- In a *forward contract,* one party agrees to buy, and the counterparty to sell, a physical asset or a security at a specific price on a specific date in the future. If the future price of the asset increases, the buyer (at the older, lower price) has a gain, and the seller has a loss.
- A *futures contract* is a forward contract that is standardized and exchange-traded. Futures contracts differ from forward contracts in that futures are traded in an active secondary market, are regulated, are backed by the clearinghouse, and require a daily settlement of gains and losses.
- A *swap* is equivalent to a series of forward contracts. In the simplest swap, one party agrees to pay the short-term (floating) rate of interest on some principal amount, and the counterparty agrees to pay a certain (fixed) rate of interest in return. Swaps of different currencies and equity returns are also common.
- An option to buy an asset at a particular price is termed a *call option.* The seller of the option has an *obligation* to sell the asset at the agreed-upon price, if the call buyer chooses to exercise the right to buy the asset.
- An option to sell an asset at a particular price is termed a *put option.* The seller of the option has an *obligation* to purchase the asset at the agreed-upon price if the put buyer chooses to exercise the right to sell the asset.

 ©2011 Kaplan, Inc.

FORWARD MARKETS AND CONTRACTS

Forward Contracts

A *deliverable* forward contract for an asset specifies that the long will pay a certain amount at a specific future date to the short, who will deliver the underlying asset. Neither party pays at contract initiation.

A *cash settlement* forward contract does not require actual delivery of the underlying asset, but instead requires a cash payment to the party that is disadvantaged by the difference between the market price of the asset and the contract price at the settlement date.

Early termination of a forward contract can be accomplished by entering into a new forward contract with the opposite position, at the then-current forward price. This early termination will fix the amount of the gains or losses on the forward contract as of the termination date.

Forward contracts are described by the type of asset that must be purchased or sold under the terms of the contract. Equity forwards require delivery or cash settlement based on the value of a stock, a specific portfolio of stocks, or a stock index.

Currency forwards are widely used to hedge exchange rate risk and require delivery of a specified amount of a particular currency with a contract price in another currency.

Bond forwards are often written on zero-coupon bonds with payoffs to the long that increase if rates decrease. A related type of forward contract is a forward rate agreement, where increasing rates increase the payoff to the long position.

Forward Rate Agreements

A *forward rate agreement* (FRA) can be viewed as a forward contract to borrow/lend money at a certain rate at some future date, although it is a cash settlement contract. The long position in an FRA is the party that would borrow the money (long the loan with the contract "price" being the interest rate on the loan). If the floating rate at contract expiration is above the rate specified in the forward agreement, the long position will profit; the contract can be viewed as the right to borrow at below-market rates.

The London Interbank Offered Rate (LIBOR) is a short-term rate based on the rates at which large London banks will lend U.S. dollars to each other. *Euribor* is a similar rate for borrowing and lending in euros.

The payment at settlement on an FRA is the present value of the difference in interest costs between a riskless loan at the market rate and one made at the rate specified in the contract. The difference in rates is multiplied by the notional amount of the contract to get the difference in interest due at the end of the loan term. Because this hypothetical loan would be made at contract settlement, the interest savings or excess interest costs would be paid later, at the end of the loan term. For this reason, the payment at settlement is the present value of the interest difference, discounted at the rate prevailing at settlement.

The general formula for the payment to the long at settlement is:

$$(\text{notional principal}) \left[\frac{(\text{floating rate at settlement} - \text{forward rate})\left[\frac{\text{days}}{360}\right]}{1 + \text{floating rate at settlement}\left[\frac{\text{days}}{360}\right]} \right]$$

FUTURES MARKETS AND CONTRACTS

Key Differences Between Futures and Forwards

Forwards	Futures
Private contracts	Exchange-traded
Unique customized contracts	Standardized contracts
Default risk is present	Guaranteed by clearinghouse
Little or no regulation	Regulated
No margin deposit required	Margin required and adjusted

Margin

There are three types of futures margin: initial, maintenance, and variation.

The first deposit is called the *initial margin*. Initial margin must be posted before any trading takes place. Initial margin is fairly low and equals about one day's maximum fluctuation in the contract value. The margin requirement is low because at the end of every day there is a *daily settlement* process called marking to market.

In *marking to market*, any losses for the day are removed from the trader's account, and any gains are added to the trader's account. Thus, any gains or losses in the value of the futures position (futures contract) are realized each day.

If the margin balance in the trader's account falls below a certain level (called the *maintenance margin*), the trader will get a *margin call* and must deposit more

©2011 Kaplan, Inc.

cash or securities (called the *variation margin*) into the account to bring the margin balance back up to the initial level. If the margin balance increases above the initial margin amount, the investor can withdraw funds from the account in the amount of the excess above the initial margin requirement.

Futures Contract Basics

Futures contracts specify the quality and quantity of the underlying asset, the delivery or settlement date in the future, and the place of delivery. The futures exchange decides which contracts will be traded, determines the minimum price change, and sets limits on daily price moves.

The Futures Clearing Corporation specifies margin requirements and acts as the counterparty to every trade. Standardization makes the futures contracts quite liquid, so to close out a futures position prior to settlement, a trader can just enter into an opposite futures position. The cumulative mark to market in the futures account will have already accounted for any gains or losses on the position prior to the date of the *offsetting* or *closing trade*.

Most futures contracts are terminated by offsetting trades. Delivery of the asset, cash settlement at contract expiration, or an off-exchange delivery called *exchange for physicals* are the other methods of terminating a futures position.

Some bond futures contracts provide valuable delivery options to the short that include what bond to deliver and when to deliver during the expiration month.

OPTION MARKETS AND CONTRACTS

Terminology and Basics

Call option:

- Long position: *right to buy* the underlying stock at a specific price on a future date.
- Short position: *obligation to sell* the stock to the buyer of the call option.

Put option:

- Long position: *right to sell* the underlying stock at a specific price on a future date.
- Short position: *obligation to buy* the stock from the buyer of the put option.

The *strike price (X)* represents the exercise price specified in the contract.

The seller or short position in an options contract is sometimes referred to as the *writer* of the option.

Level I and II Refresher

Stock options are typically on 100 shares of stock.

American options allow the owner to exercise the option at any time before or at expiration.

European options can only be exercised at expiration. For two otherwise identical options, an American option has more flexibility than the European option, so it is worth at least as much and typically more.

Moneyness and Intrinsic Value

An option that would provide a positive payoff if exercised is said to be *in-the-money*. The *intrinsic value* of an option is the amount that it is in-the-money, and zero otherwise. The difference between the price of an option (called its premium) and its intrinsic value is termed its *time value*.

The following table summarizes the moneyness of options based on the stock's current price, S, and the option's exercise strike price, X.

Moneyness	Call Option	Put Option
In-the-money	$S > X$	$S < X$
At-the-money	$S = X$	$S = X$
Out-of-the-money	$S < X$	$S > X$

- In general, an option is more valuable when its time to expiration is longer and when the price of the underlying asset is more volatile.
- Call options increase in value when the asset price increases, the exercise price is lower, or when the risk-free rate is higher.
- Put options increase in value when the asset price is lower, the exercise price is higher, or when the risk-free rate is lower.
- Both put and call options have greater value when the volatility of the price of the underlying asset is greater.

Interest Rate Options vs. Forward Rate Agreements (FRAs)

For interest rate options, the exercise price is an interest rate, and payoffs depend on a reference rate, such as LIBOR. Interest rate options are similar to FRAs because there is no deliverable asset and they are settled in cash, in an amount based on a notional amount and the difference between the strike rate and the reference rate.

The combination of a long interest rate call option plus a short interest rate put option has the same payoff as an FRA. One difference is that interest rate option payoffs are made after the option expiration date at a date corresponding to the end of the loan period specified in the contract (30-day LIBOR, 60-day LIBOR,

©2011 Kaplan, Inc.

90-day LIBOR, etc.). Recall that FRAs pay the present value of this interest difference at settlement.

Other Types of Options

Commodity options are on physical underlying assets, such as gold.

Index option payoffs are based on the difference between the strike price and the index, multiplied by a specified multiplier.

Options on futures give the long the right to enter into a futures position at the futures price specified in the option contract.

Minimum and Maximum Option Values

Option	Minimum Value	Maximum Value
European call	$c_t \geq \text{Max}[0,\ S_t - X\ /\ (1 + R_F)^{T-t}]$	S_t
American call	$C_t \geq \text{Max}[0,\ S_t - X\ /\ (1 + R_F)^{T-t}]$	S_t
European put	$p_t \geq \text{Max}[0,\ X\ /\ (1 + R_F)^{T-t} - S_t]$	$X\ /\ (1 + R_F)^{T-t}$
American put	$P_t \geq \text{Max}[0,\ X - S_t]$	X

Put-Call Parity

Put-call parity means that portfolios with identical payoffs must sell for the same price to prevent arbitrage. A fiduciary call (composed of a call option and a risk-free bond that will pay X at expiration) and a protective put (composed of a share of stock and a long put) both have identical payoffs at maturity. Based on this fact and the law of one price, we can state the following, for European options:

$$C + X\ /\ (1 + R_F)^T = S + P$$

Each of the individual securities in the put-call parity relationship can be expressed as:

$$S = C - P + X\ /\ (1 + R_F)^T$$

$$P = C - S + X\ /\ (1 + R_F)^T$$

$$C = S + P - X\ /\ (1 + R_F)^T$$

$$X\ /\ (1 + R_F)^T = S + P - C$$

The single securities on the left-hand side of the equations all have exactly the same payoffs at expiration as the portfolios on the right-hand side. The portfolios on the right-hand side are the *synthetic* equivalents of the securities on the left. Note that the options must be European style, and the puts and calls must have the same exercise prices for these relations to hold.

The four relations all must hold to prevent arbitrage; if there is a profitable arbitrage opportunity, *all of these relations* will be violated. If the equality does not hold, buy the *cheap* side of the equation and sell the other *expensive* side. This will produce an immediate *arbitrage profit*.

SWAP MARKETS AND CONTRACTS

One way to view a swap contract is as an exchange of loans. A simple fixed-for-floating rate swap is equivalent to one party borrowing from another at a fixed rate and the other party borrowing the same amount from the first party and paying a floating rate of interest on the loan. If the loans are in different currencies, it's a currency swap; if one of the loans requires the payment of a rate determined by the return on a stock, portfolio, or index, it is termed an equity swap.

Characteristics of Swap Contracts

- No payment required by either party at initiation except the principal values exchanged in currency swaps.
- Custom instruments.
- Not traded in any organized secondary market.
- Largely unregulated.
- Default risk is a critical aspect of the contracts.
- Institutions dominate.

Methods of Terminating a Swap

- Mutual termination.
- Offsetting swap contract.
- Resale to a third party.
- Exercising a swaption—an option to enter into an offsetting swap.

Currency Swaps

In a *currency swap*, one party makes payments denominated in one currency, while the payments from the counterparty are made in a second currency. Typically, the notional amounts of the contract, expressed in both currencies, are exchanged at contract initiation and returned at the contract termination date in the same amounts. The periodic interest payments in each of the two currencies can be based on fixed or floating rates.

 ©2011 Kaplan, Inc.

The cash flows that would occur in a currency swap are as follows:

- Unlike an interest rate swap, the notional principal actually changes hands at the beginning of the swap.
- Interest payments are made without netting. *Full interest payments in two different currencies are exchanged at each settlement date.*
- At the termination of the swap agreement (maturity), the counterparties return the notional amounts. *Notional principal is swapped again at the termination of the agreement.*

Plain Vanilla Interest Rate Swaps

The *plain vanilla interest rate swap* involves trading fixed-interest-rate payments for floating-rate payments (paying fixed and receiving floating).

The parties involved in any swap agreement are called the *counterparties.*

- The counterparty that wants variable-rate interest agrees to pay fixed-rate interest and is, therefore, called the pay-fixed side of the swap.
- The counterparty that receives the fixed payment and agrees to pay variable-rate interest is called the receive-fixed or pay-floating side of the swap.

Let's look at the cash flows that occur in a plain vanilla interest rate swap.

- Because the notional principal swapped is the same for both counterparties and is denominated in the same currency units, there is no need to actually exchange the cash.
- The determination of the variable interest rate is at the beginning of the settlement period, and the cash interest payment is made at the end of the settlement period. This is called payment in *arrears.* Because the interest payments are in the same currency, there is no need for both counterparties to actually transfer the cash. The difference between the fixed-rate payment and the variable-rate payment is calculated and paid to the appropriate counterparty. *Net interest is paid by the party who owes it.*
- At the conclusion of the swap, only the final net payment is made, because the notional principal was not swapped.

Swaps are a zero-sum game. What one party gains, the other party loses.

Interest Rate Swap Terminology

- The time frame covered by the swap is called the *tenor* of the swap.
- The *settlement dates* are when the interest payments are to be made.
- The amount used to calculate the payment streams to be exchanged is called the *notional principal.*
- The floating rate quoted is generally LIBOR flat or LIBOR plus a spread.

Swap Interest Payments

The basic formula for the net fixed-rate payment in an interest rate swap is:

$$\begin{pmatrix} \text{net fixed-rate} \\ \text{payment} \end{pmatrix}_t = \begin{pmatrix} \text{swap fixed} \\ \text{rate} - \text{LIBOR}_{t-1} \end{pmatrix} \begin{pmatrix} \dfrac{\text{number of days}}{360} \end{pmatrix} \begin{pmatrix} \text{notional} \\ \text{principal} \end{pmatrix}$$

- If this number is positive, the fixed-rate payer *owes* a net payment to the floating-rate party.
- If this number is negative, then the fixed-rate payer *receives* a net payment from the floating-rate party.

In a swap, the floating-rate payment is made based on what the floating rate was at the *beginning* of the settlement period. Hence, when a swap is negotiated (beginning of first period), the net cash payment at the end of the first period is already known. However, the cash flows for all other periods are indeterminate as of the start of the swap and are based on future values of the floating rate.

FORWARD MARKETS AND CONTRACTS

A clear understanding of the sources and timing of forward contract settlement payments will enable you to be successful on this portion of the exam without depending on pure memorization of these complex formulas.

Pricing vs. Valuation of Forward Contracts

- The *price* of a forward contract is the price specified in the contract at which the long and short sides have agreed to trade the underlying asset when the contract expires.
- The *value* of a forward contract to each side is the amount of money the counterparty would be willing to pay (or receive) to terminate the contract. It's a zero-sum game, so the value of the long position is equal to the negative of the value of the short position.
- The *no-arbitrage* price of the forward contract (with a maturity of T years) is the price at which the value of the long side and the value of the short side are both equal to zero.

$$FP = S_0 \times (1 + R_F)^T$$

Forward Contract on a Stock

A stock, a stock portfolio, or an equity index may have expected dividend payments over the life of the contract. In order to price such a contract, we

©2011 Kaplan, Inc.

must either adjust the spot price for the present value of the expected dividends (PVD) or adjust the forward price for the future value of the dividends (FVD):

$$FP(\text{on a stock}) = (S_0 - PVD) \times (1 + R_F)^T = [S_0 \times (1 + R_F)^T] - FVD$$

To calculate the *value* of the long position in a forward contract on a dividend-paying stock, we make the adjustment for the present value of the remaining expected discrete dividends at time t (PVD_t) to get:

$$V_t(\text{long position on a stock}) = (S_t - PVD_t) - \left(\frac{FP}{(1+R_F)^{T-t}}\right)$$

Forward Contract on Equity Index

The dividends on an equity index are approximately continuous, so to price and value a forward contract on an equity index, use the same basic formulas with continuous compounding at the continuously compounded risk-free rate of R_F^c and assume a continuous dividend yield of δ^c.

$$FP(\text{on equity index}) = S_0 \times e^{\left(R_F^c - \delta^c\right) \times T}$$

$$V_t(\text{long position on equity index}) = \left(\frac{S_t}{e^{\delta^c \times (T-t)}}\right) - \left(\frac{FP}{e^{R_F^c \times (T-t)}}\right)$$

Forwards on Fixed-Income Securities

To calculate the no-arbitrage forward price and value on a coupon-paying bond, substitute the present value of the expected coupon payments (PVC) *over the life of the contract* for the present value of the expected dividends to get:

$$FP(\text{on fixed-income security}) = (S_0 - PVC) \times (1 + R_F)^T$$

$$V_t(\text{long position on fixed-income security}) = (S_t - PVC_t) - \left(\frac{FP}{(1+R_F)^{T-t}}\right)$$

Forward Rate Agreements (FRAs)

Basics of FRAs:

- The long position in an FRA is the party that would borrow the money (long the loan with the contract price being the interest rate on the loan).
- If LIBOR at expiration is above the rate specified in the forward agreement, the long position in the contract can be viewed as the right to borrow at below market rates and the long will receive a payment.
- If rates at the expiration date are below the then-current market rates, the short will receive a cash payment from the long. (The right to lend at *above* market rates would have a positive value.)
- The notation for FRAs is unique. For example, a 2×3 FRA is a contract that expires in two months (60 days), and the underlying loan is settled in three months (90 days). The underlying rate is 1-month (30-day) LIBOR on a 30-day loan in 60 days. A time line for a 2×3 FRA is shown in Figure 18.

Figure 18: Illustration of a 2×3 FRA

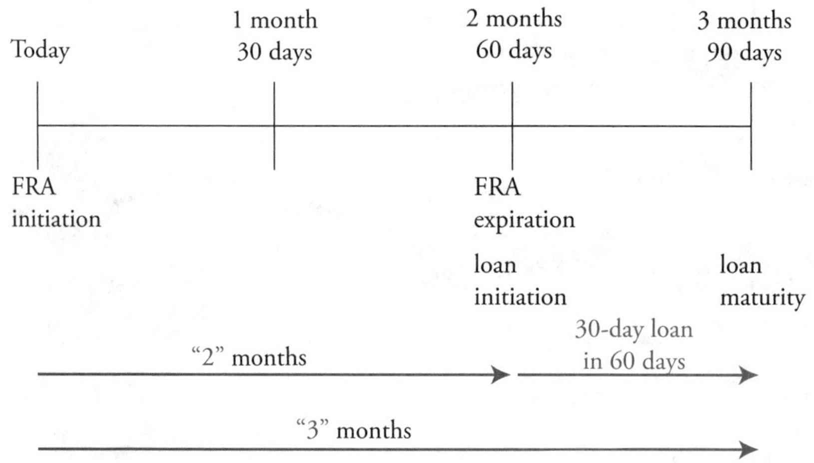

Pricing an FRA

The price of the FRA is actually the forward interest rate implied by the spot rates consistent with the FRA. For example, the price of the 2×3 FRA is the 30-day forward rate in 60 days implied by the 60- and 90-day spot rates.

Valuing an FRA

The value of an FRA to the long or short position comes from the interest savings on a loan to be made at the settlement date. This value is to be received at the end of the loan, so the value of an FRA after initiation is the present value

©2011 Kaplan, Inc.

of these savings. Just remember that if the rate in the future is less than the FRA rate, the long is obligated to borrow at above-market rates and will have to make a payment to the short. If the rate is greater than the FRA rate, the long will receive a payment from the short.

Let's outline the general steps for valuing a 2×3 FRA (a 30-day loan in 60 days) 40 days after initiation (which means there are 20 days remaining until the FRA expires).

Step 1: Calculate the implied *30-day forward rate* at the settlement date, 20 days from now, using the current 20-day spot rate and the current 50-day spot rate.

Step 2: Calculate the value of the FRA at maturity as the notional principal multiplied by the difference between the forward rate from Step 1 and the original FRA price. Make sure to convert from an annual rate to a 30-day rate. If the current forward rate is greater than the original FRA price, the long position has positive value. If the current forward rate is less than the original FRA price, the short position has positive value.

Step 3: Calculate the value of the FRA today by discounting the value at maturity from Step 2 at the 50-day spot rate.

OPTION MARKETS AND CONTRACTS

Put-Call Parity for European Options

Put-call parity must hold by arbitrage:

$$C_0 + \left[\frac{X}{(1+R_F)^T} \right] = P_0 + S_0$$

The Black-Scholes-Merton Option Pricing Model Assumptions and Limitations

The *assumptions* underlying the Black-Scholes-Merton (BSM) model are:

- The price of the underlying asset follows a lognormal distribution.
- The (continuous) risk-free rate is constant and known.
- The volatility of the underlying asset is constant and known.
- Markets are frictionless.
- The underlying asset generates no cash flows.
- The options are European.

Because of the limitations of these assumptions, the BSM model is *not appropriate*:

- For valuing interest rate options and options on bond prices because the assumption of a constant and known risk-free rate is violated.
- When the assumption of a constant and known volatility of underlying asset returns is violated.
- In cases where taxes and transactions costs are significant.
- For pricing American-style options.

Inputs to the Black-Scholes-Merton Model

There are five inputs to the BSM model: asset price, exercise price, asset price volatility, time to expiration, and the risk-free rate. The effects of changes in each input (in isolation, holding all else constant) on the value of European call and put options (on assets with no cash flows) are outlined in Figure 19.

Figure 19: BSM Sensitivities

Sensitivity Factor (Greek)	Input	Calls	Puts
Delta	Asset price (S)	Positively related delta > 0	Negatively related delta < 0
Vega	Volatility (σ)	Positively related vega > 0	Positively related vega > 0
Rho	Risk-free rate (r)	Positively related rho > 0	Negatively related rho < 0
Theta	Time to expiration (T)	Value → $0 as call → maturity theta < 0	Value usually → 0 as put → maturity theta < 0*
	Exercise price (X)	Negatively related	Positively related

* There is an exception to the general rule that European put option thetas are negative. The put value may increase as the option approaches maturity if the option is deep in the money and close to maturity.

Delta

An option's *delta* estimates the change in the value of the option for a 1-unit change in the value of the underlying stock.

$$delta_{call} = \frac{\text{change in call price}}{\text{change in stock price}}$$

©2011 Kaplan, Inc.

For small changes in stock price, a call option's delta is $N(d_1)$ from the BSM; the comparable put option's delta is $N(d_1) - 1$. The following relationships are approximations:

$$\text{change in call price} \approx N(d_1) \times \text{change in stock price}$$

$$\text{change in put price} \approx \left[N(d_1) - 1\right] \times \text{change in stock price}$$

Figure 20: Delta: Key Points to Remember

Option	Range	Far out-of-the-Money	Far in-the-Money	As Stock Price Increases
Call	0 to 1	Close to 0	Close to 1	Increases from 0 to 1
Put	−1 to 0	Close to 0	Close to −1	Increases from −1 to 0

Delta-Neutral Hedging

A *delta-neutral portfolio* is a combination of short call options with the underlying stock so that the value of the portfolio doesn't change when the value of the stock changes. The number of call options to sell to create the delta-neutral hedge is as follows:

$$\text{number of call options needed to delta hedge} = \frac{\text{number of shares hedged}}{\text{delta of call option}}$$

The delta-neutral position only holds for very small changes in the value of the underlying stock. Hence, the delta-neutral portfolio must be continuously rebalanced to maintain the hedge. This is called a *dynamic hedge*.

Gamma

Gamma measures the rate of change in delta as the underlying stock price changes. Gamma is largest when the option is at-the-money, so delta is very sensitive to changes in the underlying stock price when the option is at-the-money.

Gamma can be viewed as a measure of how poorly a dynamic hedge will perform when it is not rebalanced in response to a change in the asset price. Hedges with at-the-money options will have higher gammas, and consequently small changes in stock price will lead to large changes in delta and frequent rebalancing.

Swap Markets and Contracts

Credit Risk

Credit risk arises because of the possibility that the other party to a swap cannot or will not make the payments required by the swap contract. Several key points to remember include:

- Current credit risk is the credit risk associated with the payment currently due.
- Potential credit risk reflects the future credit risk remaining over the life of the swap.
- For an interest rate swap, potential credit risk is greatest in the middle of the swap term when the credit worthiness of the counterparty may have deteriorated since swap initiation, and there are significant payments yet to be made over the remaining term of the swap.
- For a currency swap, the maximum potential credit risk occurs after the middle of the swap term because of the remaining principal payment due at maturity.
- Credit risk can be reduced by:
  - Netting.
  - Marking to market.

Swaptions

A *payer swaption* is the right to enter into a specific swap at some date in the future as the fixed-rate payer at a rate specified in the swaption. If swap fixed rates increase (as interest rates increase), the right to enter the pay-fixed side of a swap (a payer swaption) becomes more valuable.

The value of a payer swaption at expiration (if it is in-the-money) is the present value of the difference between swap fixed-rate payments based on the higher existing swap rate and payments based on the strike rate.

A *receiver swaption* is the right to enter into a specific swap at some date in the future as the floating-rate payer at a rate specified in the swaption. A receiver swaption becomes more valuable if rates decrease.

The value of a receiver swaption at expiration (if it is in-the-money) is the present value of the difference in swap fixed-rate payments based on the higher strike rate and the lower existing swap rate.

©2011 Kaplan, Inc.

Uses of Swaptions

A swaption can be used to:

- Hedge an anticipated exposure to fixed or floating interest rate payments.
- Speculate on the direction of interest rates.
- Provide a method of exiting an existing swap prior to the normal termination date.

Swap Spread

The *swap spread* is the spread between the swap rate and the comparable maturity T-notes. The swap spread will respond to the same factors as other quality spreads.

INTEREST RATE DERIVATIVE INSTRUMENTS

Caps, Floors, and Collars

- An *interest rate cap* is an agreement in which one party agrees to pay the other at regular intervals over a certain period of time when the benchmark interest rate (e.g., LIBOR) exceeds the strike rate specified in the contract. This strike rate is called the cap rate. Because an interest rate cap is a multi-period agreement, a cap is actually a portfolio of call options on LIBOR called caplets. A long cap is also equivalent to a portfolio of long put options on fixed-income security prices.
- An *interest rate floor* is an agreement in which one party agrees to pay the other at regular intervals over a certain time period when the benchmark interest rate (e.g., LIBOR) falls below the strike rate specified in the contract. This strike rate is called the floor rate. Because a floor is a multi-period agreement, a floor is actually a portfolio of put options on LIBOR called floorlets. A long floor is also equivalent to a portfolio of long call options on fixed-income security prices.
- An *interest rate collar* is a simultaneous position in a floor and a cap on the same benchmark rate over the same period with the same settlement dates. There are two types of collars. The first type of collar is to purchase a cap and sell a floor to hedge a floating-rate liability. The second type of collar is to purchase a floor and sell a cap to hedge a floating-rate asset.

CREDIT DERIVATIVES

Characteristics and Advantages

A *credit default swap* (CDS) is essentially an insurance contract. The reference obligation is the fixed-income security on which the swap is written—usually a bond but potentially also a loan. If default occurs on the reference obligation, the buyer of the swap receives a payment from the seller. To obtain this coverage, the buyer of the swap pays the seller a premium that is either paid up front or over a period of time. The buyer of the swap is said to be buying protection, whereas the seller is said to be selling protection and assuming credit risk. The default swap premium is also referred to as the default swap spread.

The CDS creates a short position in the reference obligation for the buyer of the swap because the value of the CDS increases as the credit quality and market price of the reference obligation decline. The default swap becomes more valuable to the buyer when the reference obligation decreases in credit quality. The default swap could then be sold for a profit. Note that the CDS does not protect against market-wide interest rate risk, only credit risk.

Relative to the underlying, credit derivatives allow credit risk to be separately managed from interest rate risk, facilitate short positions, offer greater liquidity, provide customized positions, and provide confidentiality.

Uses of Credit Derivatives

- Banks use credit derivatives for hedging and regulatory purposes.
- Investment banks act as market makers, hedge exposures, and seek mispriced situations (as do hedge funds and fund managers).
- Insurance firms sell protection, and corporations use them for hedging and income enhancement.

Strategies

Credit derivatives can be used in the following strategies:
- Basis trade.
- Curve trade.
- Index trade.
- Options trade.
- Capital structure trade.
- Correlation trade.

©2011 Kaplan, Inc.

RISK MANAGEMENT

Professor's Note: Your knowledge of confidence intervals is applicable to the calculation of value at risk (VAR). You'll need to be familiar with how the measurement of VAR utilizes a one-tailed test given a normal distribution.

Confidence Intervals: Normal Distribution

A *confidence interval* is a range of values around an expected outcome within which we expect the actual outcome to occur some specified percentage of the time.

The following graph illustrates confidence intervals for a standard normal distribution, which has a mean of 0 and a standard deviation of 1. We can interpret the values on the x-axis as the number of standard deviations from the mean. Thus, for any normal distribution, we can say, for example, that 68% of the outcomes will be within one standard deviation of the mean. This would be referred to as a 68% confidence interval.

Figure 21: The Standard Normal Distribution and Confidence Intervals

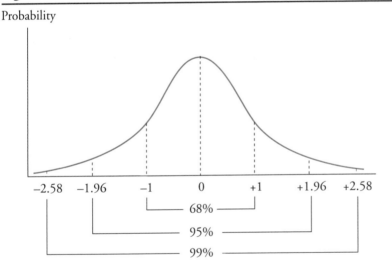

Student's *t*-Distribution

* Symmetrical (bell-shaped).
* Defined by single parameter, degrees of freedom (*df*), where df = n − 1 for hypothesis tests and confidence intervals involving a sample mean.
* *Less peaked* and *fatter tails* than a normal distribution.
* As sample size (degrees of freedom) increases, *t*-distribution approaches normal distribution.

Student's t-distribution is similar in concept to the normal distribution in that it is bell-shaped and symmetrical about its mean. The *t-distribution* is appropriate when working with small samples (n < 30) from populations with *unknown variance* and normal, or approximately normal, distributions. It may also be appropriate to use the *t*-distribution when the population variance is unknown and the sample size is large enough that the central limit theorem will assure the sampling distribution is approximately normal.

Figure 22: Student's *t*-Distribution and Degrees of Freedom

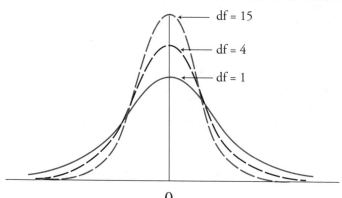

©2011 Kaplan, Inc.

INDEX

Index

©2011 Kaplan, Inc.

J

junior bonds 41
justified price multiple 30

K

key rate duration 55
k-factor model 71
kurtosis 4

L

labor productivity 13
legal and regulatory constraints 75
legal structure 53
liquidity constraints 75
liquidity preference theory 43
liquidity risk 38
London Interbank Offered Rate (LIBOR) 83

M

macroeconomic factor models 70
maintenance margin 84
margin call 84
market model 69
market portfolio 68
market segmentation theory 43
marking to market 84
modified duration 51
monetary policy 19
monetary policy tools 42
moneyness 86
mortgage-backed security (MBS) 56
mortgage passthrough security 40
multifactor models 70
multiple IRRs 35
municipal bonds 41
municipal debt 54
mutually exclusive 21

N

negative convexity 50
negative covariance 6
negative covenants 53
negative effects of regulation 14
negotiable CDs 42
net asset value 76

net operating income 78
net present value 22
nominal yield spreads 43

O

one-tailed test 11
one-third rule 14
open-end fund 76
opportunity costs 21
option-adjusted spread (OAS) 49
option markets 85, 93
options on futures 87

P

parity relationships 16
participation certificates 40
par value 36
passthrough security 56
payback period 22
payer swaption 96
PEG ratio 31
plain vanilla interest rate swap 89
political risk 54
portfolio management process 74
positive covariance 6
PRAT model 28
prepayment option 37
prepayment risk 38, 56
price-to-book (P/B) ratio 31
price value of a basis point (PVBP) 52
pricing an FRA 92
principal strips 40
probability distribution 8
profitability index 22
pro forma balance sheets 24
purchasing power parity (PPP) 16
put-call parity 87, 93
put feature 37
put option 82, 85

Q

quality of the collateral 53
quality of the servicer 53
quota 15, 16

Index

©2011 Kaplan, Inc.

Y

Z

Notes

Notes

Notes

Notes

Notes

Notes

Required Disclaimers:

CFA Institute does not endorse, promote, or warrant the accuracy or quality of the products or services offered by Kaplan Schweser. CFA Institute, CFA®, and Chartered Financial Analyst® are trademarks owned by CFA Institute.

Certified Financial Planner Board of Standards Inc. owns the certification marks CFP®, CERTIFIED FINANCIAL PLANNER™, and federally registered CFP (with flame design) in the U.S., which it awards to individuals who successfully complete initial and ongoing certification requirements. Kaplan University does not certify individuals to use the CFP®, CERTIFIED FINANCIAL PLANNER™, and CFP (with flame design) certification marks.
CFP® certification is granted only by Certified Financial Planner Board of Standards Inc. to those persons who, in addition to completing an educational requirement such as this CFP® Board-Registered Program, have met its ethics, experience, and examination requirements.

Kaplan Schweser and Kaplan University are review course providers for the CFP® Certification Examination administered by Certified Financial Planner Board of Standards Inc. CFP Board does not endorse any review course or receive financial remuneration from review course providers.

GARP® does not endorse, promote, review, or warrant the accuracy of the products or services offered by Kaplan Schweser of FRM® related information, nor does it endorse any pass rates claimed by the provider. Further, GARP® is not responsible for any fees or costs paid by the user to Kaplan Schweser, nor is GARP® responsible for any fees or costs of any person or entity providing any services to Kaplan Schweser. FRM®, GARP®, and Global Association of Risk Professionals™ are trademarks owned by the Global Association of Risk Professionals, Inc.

CAIAA does not endorse, promote, review or warrant the accuracy of the products or services offered by Kaplan Schweser, nor does it endorse any pass rates claimed by the provider. CAIAA is not responsible for any fees or costs paid by the user to Kaplan Schweser nor is CAIAA responsible for any fees or costs of any person or entity providing any services to Kaplan Schweser. CAIA®, CAIA Association®, Chartered Alternative Investment Analyst℠, and Chartered Alternative Investment Analyst Association®, are service marks and trademarks owned by CHARTERED ALTERNATIVE INVESTMENT ANALYST ASSOCIATION, INC., a Massachusetts non-profit corporation with its principal place of business at Amherst, Massachusetts, and are used by permission.

CPCU® is a registered mark owned by the American Institute for CPCU and the Insurance Institute of America.

ChFC®, Chartered Financial Consultant®, CLU®, Chartered Life Underwriter®, and CASL®, Chartered Advisor for Senior Living® are registered marks owned by The American College. Kaplan Schweser is not affiliated or associated in any way with The American College. The American College does not endorse, promote, review, or warrant the accuracy of any courses, exam preparation materials, or other products or services offered by Kaplan Schweser and does not verify or endorse any claims made by Kaplan Schweser regarding such products or services, including any claimed pass rates.